The State of Music

Virgil Thomson

The STATE *of* MUSIC

New York · 1939
William Morrow and Company

Published, November, 1939
Second printing, January, 1940

*Printed in the United States
By Quinn & Boden Company, Inc., Rahway, N. J.*

Contents

The State of Music

CHAPTER ONE

OUR ISLAND HOME, or

What it feels like to be a musician

EVERY profession is a secret society. The musical profession is more secret than most, on account of the nature of music itself. No other field of human activity is quite so hermetic, so isolated. Literature is made out of words, which are ethnic values and which everybody in a given ethnic group understands. Painting and sculpture deal with recognizable images that all who have eyes can see. Architecture makes perfectly good sense to anybody who has ever built a chicken coop or lived in a house. Scholarship, science, and philosophy, which are verbalizations of general ideas, are practiced humbly by all, the highest achievements of these being for the most part verifiable objectively by anyone with access to facts. As for politics, religion, government, and sexuality, every loafer in a pub or club has his opinions, his passions, his inalienable orientation about them. Even the classical ballet is not very different from any other stylized muscular spectacle, be that diving or tennis or bull-fighting or horse-racing or simply a military parade.

Among the great techniques, music is all by itself, an auditory thing, the only purely auditory thing there is. It is comprehensible only to persons who can remember sounds. Trained or untrained in the practice of the art, these persons are correctly called "musical." And their common faculty gives them access to a secret civilization completely impenetrable by outsiders.

The professional caste that administers this civilization is proud, dogmatic, insular. It divides up the rest of the world into possible customers and non-customers, or rather into two kinds of customers, the music-employers and the music-consumers, beyond whom lies a no man's land wherein dwells everyone else. In no man's land takes place one's private life with friends and lovers, relatives, neighbors. Here live your childhood playmates, your enemies of the classroom, the soldiers of your regiment, your chums, girl-friends, wives, throw-aways, and the horrid little family next door.

Private human life is anything but dull. On the contrary, it is far too interesting. The troublesome thing about it is that it has no real conventions, makes no inner sense. Anything can happen. It is mysterious, unpredictable, unrehearsable. Professional life is not mysterious at all. The whole music world understands music. Any musician can give to another a comprehensible rendition of practically any piece. If there is anything either of them doesn't understand, there are always plenty of people they can consult about it.

The profession rules are extremely simple. In the unwritten popular vein, or folk-style, anything goes. If a piece is written out and signed, then all the musician has to do is to execute the written notes clearly, accurately, and unhesitatingly at such a speed and with such variations of force as are demanded by the composer's indications, good common sense, and the limitations of the instrument. Inability to do this satisfactorily can be corrected by instruction and practice. The aim of instruction and practice is to enable the musician to play fast and slow and loud and soft in any known rhythm, whether of the pulsating or of the measured kind, without any non-deliberate obscurity and without any involuntary violation of the conventions of tonal "beauty" current in his particular branch of the art. The musician so prepared is master of his trade; and there are few emergencies in professional life that he cannot handle, if he still likes music.

Private life, on the other hand, is beset by a thousand insoluble crises, from unrequited love to colds in the head. Nobody, literally nobody, knows how to avoid any of them. The Christian religion itself can only counsel patience and long-suffering. It is like a nightmare of being forced to execute at sight a score much too difficult for one's training on an instrument nobody knows how to tune and before a public that isn't listening anyway.

Yet plain private life has to be lived every day. Year after year we stalk an uncharted jungle with our colleagues and our co-citizens. We fight with them for food and love and power, defending ourselves as we can, attacking when we must. The description of all that is the story-teller's job. I would not and could not compete. From the musical enclosure or stockade, all that really counts is the easy game near by, the habitual music-consumer.

Sometimes a consumer is musically literate to the point of executing string-quartets in the home. Sometimes he can't read a note. He is still a consumer if he likes music. And he likes music if he has visceral reactions to auditory stimuli.

Muscular reactions to such stimuli do not make a music-lover. Almost anybody can learn to waltz, or to march to a drum. My father and his mother before him were what used to be called "tone-deaf." They never sang or whistled or paid any attention to musical noises. The four to six hours a day piano practice that I did for some years in my father's house never fazed either of them. They would read or sleep while it was going on as easily as I read or sleep on a railway train. Their rhythmic sense, however, was intact and quite well-developed. They could even recognize a common ditty or hymn-tune, provided they knew the words, by the prosodic pattern of its longs and shorts. I do not doubt that intensive drilling could have developed their musical prowess to more elaborate achievements. Knowing their lives as I do, I doubt if either of them would have had a better life for having wasted time on an enterprise for which he had no real gift.

The music-consumer is a different animal, and commerce with him is profitable. We provide him with music; he responds with applause, criticism, and money. All are useful. When Miss Gertrude Stein remarked that "artists don't need criticism; all they need is praise," she was most certainly thinking about the solitary arts, to which she is especially sensitive, namely, easel-painting and printed poetry. The collaborative arts cannot exist without criticism. Trial and error is their *modus operandi,* whether the thing designed for execution is a railway-station, a library, a "symphonic poem," a dictionary, an airplane for transatlantic flights, or a tragedy for public performance.

Consumer-criticism and consumer-applause of music, as of architecture, are often more perspicacious than professional criticism and applause. What one must never forget about them is that the consumer is not a professional. He is an amateur. He makes up in enthusiasm what he lacks of professional authority. His comprehension is intuitive, perfidious, female, stubborn, seldom to be trusted, never to be despised. He has violent loves and rather less violent hatreds. He is too unsure for hatred, leaves that mostly to the professionals. But he does get pretty upset sometimes by music he doesn't understand.

On the whole he is a nice man. He is the waves around our island. And if any musician likes to think of himself as a granite rock against which the sea of public acclaim dashes itself in vain, okay, let him do so. That is a common fantasy. It is a false image of the truth, nevertheless, to group all the people who like listening to music into a composite character, a hydra-headed monster, known as The Public. The Public doesn't exist; there is no such animal. A given hall- or theaterful of people has its personality, of course, and its own bodily temperature, as every performer knows; but such an audience is just like any other friend to whom one plays a piece. A performance is a flirtation. Its aim is seduction. The granite-rock pose is a flirting device, nothing more. The artist who is indifferent to his audience loses that audience and comes home empty-handed from the war.

While I was growing up in Kansas City, the consumers I came in contact with were very much as I describe them here. Later, when I went to college, I encountered a special variety, the intellectual music-fancier. This is a species of customer who talks about esthetics all the time, mostly the esthetics of visual art. He views modern music as a tail to the kite of modern painting, and modern painting as a manifestation of the Modern Spirit. This is all very mystical, as you can see, and quite false. There is no Modern Spirit. There are only some modern techniques. If it were otherwise, the market prices of music and painting and poetry would not be quite so disparate as they are.

The intellectual music-fancier is useful as an advertising medium, because he circulates among advance-guard consumers. He is psychologically dangerous to musicians, however, because he insists on lecturing them about taste. He assumes to himself, from no technical vantage point, a knowledge of musical right and wrong; and he is pretty sacerdotal about dispensing that knowledge. He is not even a professional critic, responsible to some publication with a known intellectual or advertising policy. He is likely to have some connection with the buying or selling of pictures. He is a snob in so far as he is trying to get something without paying for it, climbing at our expense. And his climb is very much at our expense if we allow him to practice his psychological black magic on us, his deadly-upas-tree rôle, in the form either of positive criticism or of a too-impressive negation. On the whole, he is not as nice a man as the less intellectual consumer; and he must be handled very firmly indeed.

In dealing with employers, professional solidarity, lots of good will, and no small amount of straight human forbearance are necessary. Musicians back-stage quarrel a good deal among themselves. They practically always present a united front to the management. It isn't that one dislikes the management especially, or disapproves of his existence. He is simply a foreigner. On the job to be done, he just doesn't speak our language.

Verbal communication about music is impossible except among musicians. Even among them there is no proper language. There is only technical jargon plus gesture. The layman knows neither convention. He cannot gesture about another man's trade, because a trade's sign language is even more esoteric than its jargon. If he knows a little of either, communication merely becomes more difficult, because both jargon and sign language have one meaning for the outside world, a dictionary meaning if you like, and five hundred meanings for the insider, hardly one of which is ever the supposed or dictionary meaning. The musician and his employer are like an Englishman and an American, or like a Spaniard and an Argentine. They think they are differing over principles and disliking each other intensely, when they are really not communicating at all. For what they speak, instead of being one language with different accents, as is commonly supposed, is really two languages with the same vocabulary. The grammar is the same grammar and the words are the same words, but the meanings are not the same meanings. The plain literal meanings of words like pie, lamb, and raspberry are different enough between America and the British Isles. For an inhabitant of either country even to suspect what the other fellow means by general words like gratitude, love, loyalty, revenge, and politeness requires years of foreign residence.

So it is between us and our non-musical collaborators. Preachers and theatrical directors, for instance, will practically always ask you to play faster when they mean louder; and they get into frightful tempers at what they think is a too-loud background for a prayer or soliloquy. Nine times out of ten the musician is playing just this side of inaudibility and is killing the effect not by playing noisily but by playing *espressivo*. He thinks an expressive scene needs an expressive accompaniment. It rarely occurs to him, unless told, to play *senza espressione.* He doesn't mind playing so when told, because the *senza espressione* is a legitimate, though rarish, musical effect. It just doesn't occur to him usually.

It is impossible, however, for a layman to ask a musician to play without expression. He can demand a little less agony when the player gets clean out of hand, but that is as far as he can think technically. Even if he knows the term *senza espressione,* he imagines it to mean "in a hard-boiled, mechanical manner," which it doesn't. To musicians it means "without varying noticeably the established rhythm or the dynamic level." It is far from a hard-boiled or mechanical effect. It is a very refined effect, particularly useful for throwing into relief the expressive nature of whatever it accompanies.

Film-directors are particularly upsetting to the musician, because, dealing with photography as they do, they live in constant fear lest music, the stronger medium, should hog the show. At the same time, they want it to hog the show whenever the show shows signs of falling apart. They expect you, wherever the story is unconvincing or the continuity frankly bad, to deceive the audience by turning on a lot of insincere hullabaloo. Now insincerity on the part of actors and interpreters is more or less all right, but insincere authorship leads to no good end.

Theater people and musicians all know this. Film people do not seem to. For all the skill and passion that have gone into the making of movies, the films are still a second-rate art form, like mural painting, because they try to convince us of characters and motivations that their own authors do not believe in, and because they refuse a loyal co-operation with music, their chief aid, choosing naïvely to use the more powerful medium as whitewash to cover up the structural defects of the weaker. It takes lots of tact and persistence to pull off a creditable job in such an industry.

The most successful users of music are the concert organizers. They confine themselves to saying yes and no. The workman never has much trouble with an employer who knows what he doesn't want. On the contrary, negation simplifies everything; and one can then proceed by elimination. What gives a musician the jitters is positive criticism, being told in advance what the result should sound like. Such talk sterilizes him by bringing in emotive considerations (the layman's language lending more moral-value connotation to technical words than the workman's language does) at a moment when successful solution of the problem in hand, that of speaking expressively (though not necessarily *con espressione*) to a public, demands that he keep all moral values and taste-connotations out of his mind.

I am trying to tell in this roundabout way what it feels like to be a musician. Mostly it is a feeling of being different from everybody but other musicians and of inhabiting with these a closed world. This world functions interiorly like a republic of letters. Exteriorly it is a secret society, and its members practice a mystery. The mystery is no mystery to us, of course; and any outsider is free to participate if he can. Only he never can. Because music-listening and music-using are oriented toward different goals from music-making, and hence nobody really knows anything about music-making except music-makers. Everybody else is just neighbors or customers, and the music world is a tight little island entirely surrounded by them all.

CHAPTER TWO

THE NEIGHBORS, or

Chiefly about painters and painting

IT IS not healthy for musicians to live too close to the confraternity. The white light of music is too blinding, and professional jealousies are a fatigue. One needs friends of another mind. A great deal of my own life seems to have been passed among painters. My sister, who was ten years older than I, was a china-painter. She earned a good living at it and paid for my music lessons, bought me my first piano. The house was full always of her colleagues and customers and the blessed odor of turpentine. To this day that resinous acridity seems to me the normal atmosphere for music to breathe and grow in.

Perhaps that is why Paris, where one is surrounded by painters, has always reminded me of Kansas City; and no doubt that is why I feel at home there. Because Paris contains, or did some years ago, by census, sixty thousand artist-painters earning their living at their trade. Believe it or not, sixty thousand professional easel-painters. Naturally one is surrounded by them. And a pleasant lot they are too, cheerful and healthy and leading regular lives.

Not orderly lives, by any means, because disorder, both material and moral, is of the essence in a painter's life. Their incomes and their love-lives are as jumpy as a fever chart. Their houses are as messy as their palettes. They view life as a multiplicity of visible objects, all completely different. A dirty towel in the middle of the floor, wine-spots on the piano keys, a hairbrush in the butter plate are for them just so many light-reflecting surfaces. Their function is to look at life, not to rearrange it. All of which, if it makes for messiness in the home, also makes for ease in social intercourse. This plus the fact that they all have perfectly clear consciences after four o'clock, or at whatever hour the daylight starts giving out.

The painter's whole morality consists of keeping his brushes clean and getting up in the morning. He wakes up with the light, tosses till the sun is overhead, then gets up and starts moving around. He works moving around. Drawing, engraving, and water-color sketching can be done seated. But oil painting must be done on foot, walking back and forth. It entails no inconsiderable amount of mild physical exercise and that among turpentine fumes, which keep the lungs open. Hence your painter is on the whole a healthy and a cheerful man. His besetting maladies are digestive, due to poverty, irregular meals, and undernourishment. He requires lots of food. In middle and later life he sometimes has rheumatism. But he is seldom too ill to paint.

As soon as the light goes bad his painting day is over. He thereupon refreshes his mind by making love to his model or by quarreling with his wife, and goes out. From four till midnight he is gay and companionable. After midnight he is disagreeable, because he knows he should be in bed. It is chiefly after midnight that he takes to alcohol, when he takes to it at all. He is a man of moderate habits, abundant physical energy, and a lively though not scholarly mind. (He doesn't like to tire his eyes by sustained reading.) He has social charm, generosity (except about other painters), and a friendly indifference to music that is a constant refreshment for musicians. Unseduced by the mere charm of sounds, unimpressed by the ingenuities of musical workmanship and the triumphs of voluntary stylization, he goes straight to the heart of the matter when he goes in for music at all. He will sometimes tell you in five words what a piece is all about, a thing no musician ever knows and no music lover ever even tries to know.

He is usually non-political, though his ways are democratic. He resides among the poor, visits in châteaux, and walks unscathed through the intrigues of the literary cenacles. He makes love to princesses as if they were housemaids and to housemaids as if they were princesses, accepting service and presents from both. He has no class hatred because he has no class. He combines the ferocious independence of the solitary intellectual with the dignity of the skilled manual worker.

He bands together for aesthetic purposes much more frequently than for economic. Unlike the musician, who is a union man and a petty bourgeois with an organized orientation in class-struggle tactics and consequently a tendency toward political affiliations (he is usually either a Third-International Communist or an extreme-right reactionary); unlike the poet, who has an over-elaborate education and no economic place in society at all and who tends hence to shoot the works politically by attaching his unrequited social passions to some desperate and recondite cause like Catalan autonomy, Anglo-Catholicism, or the justification of Leon Trotsky; unlike the sculptors and the architects, who in order to function at all must pass their lives in submission among politicos and plutocrats; unlike the doctors, the scholars, and the men of science, who are a whole social class to themselves, and who function as a united political party for the maintenance of that strangle-hold on the educational system which they acquired during the nineteenth century; unlike the manufacturers and the merchants, who know their cops and their aldermen and who always vote (to say the least); unlike actors and theater people, who, whether poor or prosperous, are irresponsible vagabonds, but who do have a trade-union of sorts and an enormous class solidarity; the painter is a man of no fixed economic orientation, no class feeling, and very little professional organization of any kind.

Since the abolition of the guilds by the French Revolution, no painters' union or academy has ever been seriously effective. (Similarly, no dealers' consortium or trust has ever squeezed the painter economically.) The British Royal Academy is little more than a Kiwanis club or a Fifth Avenue Merchants' Association. The painters don't even run an educational institution of any dependable kind. They refuse to systematize anything. There is some virtue in this refusal. Alone among all the higher skills, painting is still learned rather than taught. In the state-endowed academies, in the private ateliers, in art students' leagues, in life classes at provincial museums, oil painting and its allied techniques are considered by students and instructors alike to be progressively acquired skills rather than a corpus of esoteric knowledge progressively administered. Even the Dynamic Symmetry racket, which is an attempt to subject easel-painting, so recently free from their domination, to the ancient rules of decorative design, must eventually be submissive to the judgment of the Seeing Eye.

The Seeing Eye has no opinions. A still-life, a nude, a landscape (no matter what sentimental tie-up may be involved in the painter's choice of subject), is exactly what the painter puts down and what any beholder sees when he looks at it. Very little more is involved. The painter's technique, however complete, however analytic, can only describe particular objects. It is incapable of stating a general idea or of depicting the emotional, the utilitarian value of anything. Hence the great moral freedom of painters as a race. They keep a cleaner separation than any other kind of man I know between their lives and their works, even, in their work, between vision and execution. Their vision is personal and subjective, their rendering of it precise, objective, non-emotional. All the emotional things like sexuality, politics, elegance, family life, and religion are kept strictly in the background of their lives as private games, subjects for talk, indulgences for the darker hours of the day.

They can accept without mental trickery the dictates of fashion and of politics about what fashion and politics think is appropriate subject-matter for painting, especially if large commissions are involved. What do they care whether their model is supposed to represent Jesus Christ or Lucifer or Love in Idleness or Mr. John Rockefeller or The Conquest of Tahiti or The Workingman Triumphant or Agriculture Shaking Hands with the Machine-Age? He is just a model to them. And the drapery is just so many varied textures, each reflecting light in its own way to the Seeing Eye. An apple, a banknote, a pair of buttocks, all is one to them, because all is infinite multiplicity.

Mark you, my portrait of The Painter is of the ideal, or rather the average painter, the easel-painter as he exists among his sixty thousand brethren in Paris. The painter in isolation is another man. If you take him out of his water and put him on an island somewhere, out of the reach of other painters and with no access to a picture merchant, or if you send him to teach in some provincial agglomeration where there is no rivalry and no market, he goes very bad indeed. All alone he must cover the social gamut. He must drink and make merry and change wives and raise children; he must go to cock-fights and gamble and collect folk-lore and spend money; he must patronize the local whore-house and picket the local pants factory and waste his eyes reading books. It is too big a job. If the booze doesn't get him, the bourgeoisie must. A sad man indeed is the painter exiled from his kind.

An embittered man is the painter who over-indulges

in applied art. Patterns, posters, costumes, theater, the painter does better than the specialists. Because where the specialists have only a bag of tricks, the painter has some hard-earned general knowledge about color, light, proportion, and arrangement for high visibility. He enjoys making applications of this knowledge, playing new tricks on old trades, giving everything style, getting paid for it. The indulgence is a pleasant one indeed. The effects of over-indulgence are emptiness, staleness, sterility, and bad temper.

Even the much-admired virtuoso-skills allied to oil painting should not be indulged in any more than is necessary to prove that one can do them if one has to. The etching, the dry-point, the silver-point, the water-color are too pretty to be much good. It is easy to do them with charm, well-nigh impossible to give them any force. Preoccupation with such minor matters is the mark of a painter who is trying to go commercial respectably or professorial with impunity.

Commissioned portrait painting is also a deviation. Because the problems of painting are three and only three: animate objects, inanimate objects, and scenery. The sum-up of them all is the licentious picnic (the landscape with draped figures, undraped figures, and food). The portrait that isn't ordered is perfectly legitimate. It is just a draped figure, and resemblance doesn't matter. But facial resemblance, which is what people pay for in paid portraits, is outside the canon of painting. It is a trick, a gift. It cannot be learned or taught. The painter who can pull it off steadily seldom pays much attention to the serious problems of painting. Doesn't have to, because resembling portraiture is well paid. He is ashamed, though, because he is held in low esteem by his kind. Moreover, that psychic intimacy with the sitter that is necessary for the execution of good portraiture is upsetting to the nervous system and undermines character; also the continuous frequenting of politicians and of the rich that are necessary both to get portrait-commissions and to execute them is in itself a full-time occupation and not a very noble one.

As for mural painting, only second-raters ever do it a second time. The only special technique involved is the getting of jobs. Excellent painting can perfectly well be done on a wall, of course, or on a ceiling. It can be done on a bar-mirror in epsom salts, on a candy-box, on the back of a hairbrush, or around the legs of a piano. It must always be an image, it must depict something, however abstractly. It must create an illusion. If it sacrifices representation to anything else it is decorative design; and that is another man's trade. The real trouble about large-scale mural painting in our epoch is that unless it is executed in a precious material, in which case it is not free-hand painting but something else, it must inevitably compete with other large-scale paid-advertising in color, that is to say, electric signs and billboards. In consequence, it tends towards blatancy and over-simplification and thus fails to profit by those fuller resources of the painter's technique the deployment of which would be his only legitimate excuse for being engaged in paid-advertising at all.

There is no way around it. The painter who doesn't paint pictures is a routine man and a bore. The painter who is predominantly an easel-painter is a noble animal and a charming neighbor. He is the type-practitioner in our age of the arts both beautiful and liberal. This has not always been so. The seventeenth century had its priests and preachers whom it counted on for inspiration, as well as for the work of the world; these directed the religious wars and the colonial expansions, the exploration of three continents and the taming of wild folk. The eighteenth had its philosophers and journalists, its generalizing men of letters, counted on them for social guidance and for prophecy. The nineteenth century sucked its vitality for industrial and business expansion out of poets, musicians, and scientists. Big business today lives on the calculators and the mathematical physicists, while the arts of music and literature, completely divorced from the realities of supra-national co-operation, fecundate in a vacuum, drawing their moral support in this depressing enterprise from the only really classless man there is, the painter, and leaving to him in turn the center of the world's artistic stage, as well as the privilege of collecting most of the receipts.

The depiction of the visible world might well have been left to him too, did not journalism and photography cover the ground more thoroughly. As a matter of fact, painting and photography work very well side by side, just as poetry and journalism go hand in hand and often hand in glove. The boom in oil painting that has lasted from 1860 on, from the Pre-Raphaelites and the Impressionists through the Cubists, Surrealists, and Neo-Romantics, is exactly contemporary with the rise of commercial photography. Photography has taken over from painting nearly that whole mass of boring and fastidious work that is represented by illustration, documentation, and personal portraiture. Both arts have prospered in consequence.

But with all the photography that goes on in the world, one might expect the photographers themselves to be more in evidence than they are. I must say they are fairly noticeable in Germany, which is the ancestral home of The Toy, her modern form of toy-consciousness being a passion for optical instruments and for playing with them in public. Elsewhere, although everybody knows a photographer or two, one is rarely surrounded by them as one is surrounded by painters in Paris, by men of letters in London, by musicians, I imagine, in Vienna, certainly by school-teachers in Boston and by journalists in New York.

They are strange little men, photographers, always a bit goofy and incommunicable. They live on idiosyncratic observation, on fancy. Practicing the most objective technique known to art, they cherish a secluded and violent life of the imagination. They are sad, pensive, and introverted. They lead their lives in rain-coats. They have bad complexions and are riddled with chronic diseases, usually of nervous origin.

Journalists are plentiful everywhere and entertaining too, full of jokes and stories. Only their jokes are not very funny and their stories are inexact. Their information is always incomplete, because nobody ever tells them the truth about anything. Their philosophy of life and art and their technique of expression are incurably, dogmatically superficial. Their private lives are full of banal melodrama. They are, to a man, either dyspeptic or alcoholic or both. They must be avoided in bands, because they bring out the worst in one another. Singly they are fun but rather indigestible.

As for the sculptors and the architects, they are a pretty negligible company. The former are personally vain and professionally pretentious. They are troublesome when they turn up; but they turn up rarely nowadays, their art being in decline. The latter exist in abundance but are tame and lacking in savor. They frequent the rich and are impressed. They marry above them and send their children to schools they can't afford. They are good enough neighbors; they will always lend you a cup of olive oil. But there is no real sustenance in them.

Theatrical people are better. They are ostentatious and repetitive, but they have a childish playfulness and a complete lack of grown-up morality that are refreshing. They are superb in times of financial depression. In the long run, of course, they are unfrequentable on account of their late working-hours, just as vocalists are unfrequentable because they are always having to go to bed. The latter are companionable and good cooks (I count them among the non-musical neighbors because, as everybody knows, they are mostly not very musical), but they are neurotic. They can't drink or smoke or stay up after ten o'clock without worrying about themselves. And they are completely commercial-minded. Dancers are auto-erotic and have no conversation.

No, seriously, it is the painters who by their numbers, by their charm and healthiness, and by their unique social freedom, have imposed upon the twentieth century their own type as the model of what an artist should be like. If all art in Walter Pater's day could be said to "aspire to the condition of music," all artists, certainly all artists today, aspire to the condition of the painter, envying him his peaceful and regular life, his cheerfulness and his fecundity, his vigorous physical energies, his complete lack of emotional complexity, and (among the higher-flight ones) certainly, yes very certainly, his income.

CHAPTER THREE

SURVIVALS OF AN EARLIER CIVILIZATION, or

Shades of poets dead and gone

POETRY is the oldest of the arts and the most respected. The musical tradition we practice has scarcely a thousand years. Architecture, sculpture, and decorative design have passed since ancient times through so many esthetic revolutions that very little is left in them of any authoritative tradition. Improvisational one-man easel-painting in oil (painting as we know it) dates barely from the seventeenth century.

Poetry, as we know it, goes straight back to the Greeks and to the Hebrew children. There has been no interruption for twenty-five hundred years in the transmission of its technical procedures, no hiatus in the continuity of its comprehension by the literate classes of Europe. It has survived changes in religion, political revolutions, the birth and death of languages. Its classic masters enjoy a prestige scarcely exceeded by that of the Holy Evangelists. By populace and scholars alike they are admired above confessors and martyrs, priests, prophets, historians, psychologists, romancers, and ethical guides, and far above statesmen or soldiers, orators or newshawks. For they and their heirs are the recognized masters of the most puissant of all instruments, the word.

The poetic prestige remains, but the poetic function has contracted. As champions of the arts of love, poets made war for centuries on the Christian Church and won. As analysts of its motivations and as experts of amorous device, they were the undisputed masters of that subject till Sigmund Freud, a nerve doctor, beat them at it in our own day. (Karl Marx, a nineteenth-century economist, had already beaten them at social analysis and at political prophecy.) With love now the specialty (in every aspect) of the medical profession, with government (both past and future) better understood by sectarian political groups and better explained by journalists, with dramaturgy better practiced in Hollywood and Joinville, and story-telling done more convincingly by the writers of police-fiction, what is there left for the poet to do that might even partially justify his hereditary prestige?

He could retreat into "pure" poetry, of course; and he

often tries to. Much good may it do him. Because the sorry truth is there is no such refuge. In recent years the poets have talked a good deal about "purity." I am not sure what they mean by "pure" poetry, unless they mean poetry without a subject-matter; and that means exactly nothing.

Music and painting can exist perfectly well without a subject-matter, at least without any obvious or stated subject-matter. Painting of this kind is called "abstract." Musicians used to distinguish between "program" music and "absolute" music. The latter term meant music without a literary text or any specific illustrative intention, that is to say, instrumental music of an introspective nature. Neither "abstract" painting nor "absolute" music is any "purer" than any other kind of painting or music, and no painter or musician ever pretends it is. It is merely more obscure. When painters speak of "purity of line," they mean a complete lack of obscurity. When they speak of a "pure" color, they mean a shade that is unequivocal. Say an artist's intentions are "pure," if you must. That means he is not commercial-minded. The word *pure* cannot possibly have any meaning when applied to the content or structure of literature. Poetry could be pure only if it could be devoid of meaning, which it can't. You can make nonsense poetry, certainly; you can dissociate and reassociate words. But you cannot take the meanings out of words; you simply can't. You can only readjust their order. And nobody can or ever does write poetry without a subject.

What subjects, then, are available to the poet today? Practically none. Money, political events, heroism, science, mathematical logic, crime, the libido, the sexual variations, the limits of personality, the theory of revolution: the incidents of all these are more graphically recited by journalists, the principles better explained by specialists. There really isn't much left for the heirs of Homer and Shakespeare to do but to add their case-histories to the documentation of introspective psychology by the practice of automatic writing. Highly trained in linguistics (though the philologists are not bad at that either) and wearing the mantle of the Great Tradition, admired unreasonably and feared not unreasonably (for they are desperate men), they still have, as poets, no civil status, no social function, no serious job to do, and no income.

They haven't even any audience to speak of. For some time now they have been depending mainly on one another for applause. Hence the pretentiousness and the high intellectual tone of all they write. I mean that for fifty years poetry has mostly been read by other poets, and that for a good thirty years now has mostly been written to be read by other poets.

The impasse is complete. Contemporary civilization has no place for the poet save one of mere honor. Science, learning, journalism, fiction, religion, magic, and politics, all his ancient bailiwicks, are closed to him formally and completely. He is allowed to render small services to these now and then as a disseminator of existing knowledge. He is always regarded, however, by the specialists as a possible betrayer; and consequently at no time is he allowed to speak of such subjects with any but a temporarily delegated authority.

His lot is a tragic one. Nothing is left him of his art but an epigone's skill and some hereditary prestige. This last is still large enough to give him face in front of his co-citizens and to keep up the recruiting. It doesn't pay anything at all, of course. It won't buy a beer, a bus-fare, or a contraceptive. Nor does it prevent the darkest despair from seizing him when he is alone.

The prestige of classic poetry is enough to explain the market among cultured women for poets as lovers. I use the word market deliberately, because in these love affairs a certain amount of money nearly always changes hands. The poet who has no job and no private resources is a liability on his intimates. If he has a job, he is usually too busy working at it to take on seriously a love affair with a woman of leisure. If he has money from home, he always keeps somebody else or spends it on riotous living.

Any independent woman who gets involved with a poet had better figure that he is going to cost her something sooner or later, if only for bailing him out of night-courts.

For poets live high. When one is as poor as they, budgets make no sense and economies make no sense. Nothing makes any sense but basic luxury—eating well, drinking well, and making love. Independent and well-to-do women whose sex-mechanisms are excited by intellectual conversation are very useful indeed to poetry, provided they don't go motherly. (Poets don't care much for maternal types and they have a horror of fatherhood.) They serve the poet as muse, audience, and patroness all in one as long as they last. This isn't long usually. They get scared off by the violence of it all, as well as by the expense.

Everything the poet does is desperate and excessive. He eats like a pig; he starves like a professional beauty; he tramps; he bums; he gets arrested; he steals; he absconds; he blackmails; he dopes; he acquires every known vice and incurable disease, not the least common of which is solitary dipsomania.

All this after twenty-five, to be sure. Up to that age he is learning his art. There is available a certain amount of disinterested subvention for expansive lyrical poetry, the poetry of adolescence and early manhood. But nobody can make a grown-up career out of a facility for lyrical expansiveness. That kind of effusion is too intense, too intermittent. The mature nervous system won't stand it. At about twenty-six, the poets start looking around for some subject-matter outside themselves, something that will justify sustained execution while deploying to advantage all their linguistic virtuosity.

There is no such subject-matter available. Their training has unfitted them for the rendering of either those religious-political-and-epic or those humane-philosophical-and-dramatic subjects that were formerly the special domain of poetry. They are like certain scions of ancient families who have been brought up to look and act like aristocrats but who don't know beans about government. They even write more like heirs of the great dead than like creators of living literature. Their minds are full of noble-sounding words and a complete incomprehension of everything that takes place beyond the rise and fall of their own libidos. They cannot observe; they cannot even use words and syntax objectively. They are incurably egocentric.

This explains the high mortality, both literary and physiological, that takes place among poets around the age of thirty. Faced with a cultural as well as an economic impasse, some hang on just long enough to finish a few extended but essentially lyrical works conceived in the mid-twenties and then die of drink, dope, tuberculosis, or even plain suicide. Others, especially in England, become journalistic correspondents at twenty-six. The French tend toward the civil and consular services. Americans become pedagogues or reporters. A few marry rich widows. This last solution need not be counted as a literary mortality, because it is rarely permanent. It does get the poet over some difficult years of transition, however, without forcing him into drugs or invalidism; so that when the lady sees financial ruin approaching, the poet can and most frequently does start a new literary life, this time as a prose author with an objective method and a recognizable integration to his time and society.

For the poet who insists on remaining a poet, there is a compromise formula. He must manage to get through his youth either with a small patrimony or with enough health left to allow him to work at a regular job of some kind, preferably not connected with literature. In this case he usually settles down in the thirties to steady domesticity with a woman approaching (though never topping) his own social class and disappears into the landscape of ordinary modern life, carefully budgeting his leisure, his income, and his alcoholic intake. He keeps up his poetic correspondence (one of the strange things about poets is the way they keep warm by writing to one another all over the world) and occasionally takes part in esthetic controversy, all the while laying regularly but slowly his poetic eggs and publishing them in book form at three-to-five-year intervals. These eggs are called "poems of some length," and they essay to treat of historical or sociological subject-matter in the epic style. The manner is always essentially lyrical, however; and since lyricism without youth, without expansiveness, and without heat is a pretty sad affair, the best that can be said of these estimable efforts is that they are "the work of a mature talent," that they are "masterly," that they show a "profound feeling" for something or other. The fact remains that they are fairly ineffectual and are less read, on the whole, than his youthful works. An edition of five hundred to two thousand copies is disposed of, with luck, to libraries and bibliophiles, both of these last being collectors of poetry for its prestige-value. Sometimes the edition doesn't sell at all, in which case the publisher puts down his loss to prestige-advertising. Most publishers do a few such volumes a year, because they think it a good idea to have some poetry in the catalogue. You never know.

These middle-aged poets are just as charming as ever and much easier for peaceable persons to go about with than the young ones, because their habits are not such a strain on one's vitality. They are busy men with always time for a chat. They love to do you favors. They are good fathers, faithful husbands, and superb hosts. Once in a while they go out on an all-night binge; and their wives don't really mind, because a binge makes hubby feel like a dangerous fellow again. It builds him up to himself. And at no risk. Because he never does anything on these nights-out but sit with a crony and talk.

Poets at any age make sound friends. They are always helping you out of jams. They give you money. They respect your working hours but don't scold you when you don't work. They practice conversation as an art and friendship as a religion. I like too their violence, their fist-fights with cops, their Parisian literary wars. The displays of pure bitterness that one observes among them in England I find less invigorating, because the intensity of these seems to be due not so much to professional disagreement as to that exercise of social hatred within one's own class that seems to be the characteristic and special quality of British life just now.

I like their human warmth, their copious hospitality (however poor they may be), their tolerance about morals and their intolerance about ideas, their dignified resignation at all times. I even like their wives and their animals (for they mostly have wives and they all have cats or dogs or horses). Mostly I like their incredible and immutable loyalties. They are the last of honor and chivalry. They may be sordid sots or peaceful papas or gigolos on a leash. They imagine themselves to be knights-errant jousting before the Courts of Love. And they act accordingly, observing incomprehensibly delicate scruples, maintaining till death principles and refinements of principles that reason, common sense, and social convention have long since discarded as absurd. I knew a poet once who refused to salt his food when dining at a certain house, because, intending later to make love to the hostess, he would have considered it a breach of his obligation as a guest to attempt any violation of his host's home-life after having "eaten his salt." He was remembering, no doubt, some Arabic or medieval saw. He was not remembering that the "salt" of the precept could only have nowadays a symbolic meaning and that the food he partook of had already been salted in cooking anyway.

I like also their preoccupation with religion, the black arts, and psychoanalysis, and their complete inability to practice any of these consistently, even in an amateur way. They could, of course, if they were not, at the same time, so egocentric and so responsible to a tradition. Anybody can be clairvoyant or perform a miracle or two here and there who really wants to and who isn't afraid of the techniques. Unfortunately the techniques are all extremely dangerous to handle. That these techniques occasionally work there is, I think, no question. Illnesses, accidents, cures, and suicides, the favorable or unfavorable outcome of amorous projects and business deals, even the finding of lost objects, can be and every day are effected from a distance by interested outsiders. Prophecy is extensively carried on today through the techniques of numerology and of astrological calculation. A more active interference in other people's affairs is operated by the employment of three different kinds of technique. The hocus-pocus of medieval black art is far from uncommon, as are also the rituals of voodoo and fetich. Prayer, incantation, and trance are even commoner. Wilful exploitations of animal magnetism, of psychological domination, and of euphoric states are the bases of organized religions practicing openly. These last means are employed quite frankly in every domain of modern life, even (and by both sides) in class warfare. Organized salesmanship depends on little else, as do equally the morales of citizen armies and of militant political parties.

The poets seldom succumb to the temptation of tampering with any of these techniques, though they are not infrequently the victims of such practice by members of their own households. They don't do it themselves because the practice of poetry is exactly contrary in method to the exertion of secret or of psychological influences. Poetry is practiced today and, so far as I know, is only practiced in the manner that used to be called the tradition of Humane Letters, which is to say that it is written by one man to be read by all men and that it makes to him who reads it exactly whatever sense it would make to any other disinterested reader. Its vocabulary consists of neutral dictionary words. Magic practices, on the other hand, require the use of an emotional and hermetic vocabulary comprehensible in its full meaning only to initiates and hence effective psychologically far beyond the dictionary meanings of the words used or the normal significance of the gestures that accompany them. For all his egocentricity, the poet is not anti-social. The practice of magic, by whatever technique, is extremely anti-social, because all the techniques of it depend for their working on the breakdown of somebody's personality.

Now the barriers of personality are the highest product of culture and of biological evolution. Their erection is the *modus operandi,* and the interplay of persons and groups around them is the unique end of what almost anybody means by civilization. Naturally their destruction is anti-social and anti-cultural. And just as naturally, the poets, being the direct heirs of the oldest tradition of thought in civilization, are more aware than most men of the existence of anti-cultural practices and of the danger to all concerned of any self-indulgence in that direction.

Organized religions and organized devotion to revolutionary political ideals are rarely in the long run anti-social, though I would not say so much for high-powered salesmanship. The poet's objection to organized religions is that they are all in opposition to the intellectual tradition; they are the enemies of poetry and humane letters. And so are all enterprises that keep large groups of people united by the exploitation of animal magnetism (read "sex-appeal"), mental domination, and euphoric states. Such enterprises are, by definition, not anti-social if a large number of people is involved. They are simply anti-cultural. They may be aimed at an admirable end, and they are very tempting indeed if they seem to be about to effect political changes of a collectivist nature. But no matter how eager your poet may be to aid in the achievement of the desired end, he views with alarm any means of doing so that might render those left alive after the achieving of it mentally unfit to enjoy the thing achieved. His greatest value in revolutionary movements, for instance, is his annoyance-value, his incessant and tiresome insistence on the maintenance at all times of the full intellectual paraphernalia.

Laymen are likely to think the poets are just being fanciful when they talk about magic and sorcery. This is not so. They are talking very good sense indeed, though their terminology may be antiquated. As a matter of fact, they are the only group of men in the world that has any profound prescience about the unchaining of the dark forces that has taken place in our century. Their chief utility to us all is that they help us to fight those dark forces by the only effective means there is or ever has been. I mean the light of reason, the repetition of sage precept, and the continual application to all the dilemmas of human life of the ancient and unalterable principles of disinterested thought.

It seemed a few years ago as if psychiatry might be about to provide a bulwark against obscurantism. The number of psychiatrists and psychoanalysts who have themselves fallen for the delights of mental domination, who, by inducting their patients into a state of euphoria through which no reality can pierce, have covered up their failure to produce in these an integrated and realistic attitude toward society, the number, I say, of such physicians is too large. As venal a branch of science as that cannot be counted a bulwark of civilization. No doubt the material handled is dangerous. For the subconscious can only be plumbed by breaking down all personal barriers; there cannot be left even the curtained impersonality of the confessional. The slightest misstep in the handling of this doctor-patient intimacy produces a permanent enslavement of the patient and another scar on the already hard-boiled crust of the doctor's sensitivity. Let us charitably call such physicians "martyrs to science," like those laboratory-men who lose hands finger by finger working with radium. The intimacy of psychoanalysis is very much like radium, in fact, and like black magic too. It works, of course. But many a body and many a soul gets burned to a crisp in the process.

Poets are always getting burned; but mostly it is only their bodies that suffer, as anybody's body does who fans his youth into a flame. They rarely get burned by poetry. For the material of poetry is words, and words themselves are neutral. They only give off light. They never give off heat unless arranged in formulas. Poets hate formulas.

This is what Parisian literary wars are mostly about. They are attacks on formulas that have become powerful within the profession. The clearest statement of principle goes bad if it is repeated too often. It ceases to be a statement and becomes a slogan. It loses its clear meaning and takes on psychological power. The literary mind considers (and rightly) that any statement which carries more power than meaning is evil. War is therefore declared on the author of the statement in point, by another author, usually on some pretext of personal prestige. As the war goes on from wisecrack to manifesto to calumny, authors get involved who don't even know the original belligerents or the incidents of provocation. Everybody calls everybody else horrid names and a great deal of wit is unleashed. Then it all dies down and everybody makes up. But the formula, having now been subjected both to the light of reason and to all the thirty-two positions of ridicule, is no longer any good to anybody. Analysis and laughter have broken its back. The Demon is foiled. Demagogy is frustrated. Poetry is thereupon vigorous again and abundant till the next time a formula starts to rear its Sacred Head.

When I speak of statements that have more power than meaning, I am not referring to hermetic poetry, obscure poetry, or ordinary nonsense. These are not meaningless matters. On the contrary, they are over-full of meaning. Some poets wish to mean so many things at once that they can only write at all by the technique of multiple meaning, the most ancient of all poetic techniques, by the way, and newly come again to favor through the prestige of the physical sciences, which have made spectacular advance in our century by means of the dissociationist discipline. There is non-Aristotelian poetry just as there is non-Euclidian geometry. You cannot subject poetry to the conventions of common sense. Not, at least, if you want it to mean anything more than journalism does. There is that kind of verse, of course, too; and it sells extremely well; but it is journalistic verse for vulgar usage, fake folklore. I might cite Kipling, Edgar Guest, R. W. Service, and E. A. Robinson as successful practitioners of it. It bears the same relation to poetry that *Mighty Lak' a Rose* does to music. Nobody in the profession takes it any more seriously than that.

William Blake, Mallarmé, Gertrude Stein, and Lewis Carroll, on the other hand, however hermetic, however obscure or nonsensical, are taken very seriously indeed by the profession. They are taken as a bitter potion by many, but they are taken and taken seriously by everybody, however little any given poet may enjoy their competition. Even the plain public knows them for original masters.

There is no way out of the poet's plight. The best he can do for the present is to write poetry as if nobody were listening (a supposition not far from the truth) and to occupy the rest of the day as best he can. Earning money by writing poetry is out of the question, unless he can adapt himself to the theater, which it is not easy for him to do. The real difficulty about writing poetry is filling up the other twenty-three and a half hours a day. For, compared with the laboriousness of music writing and oil painting, there is very little real work involved in poetical composition. Lengthy reflection is involved and mental discipline and the nervous intensity of occasional concentration. But none of these takes time out of a man's life. The mind prepares itself in secret, underneath life's surface occupations. Putting down the result on paper is no job at all compared to the stroke-by-stroke improvisation of an oil-painting or the note-by-note inditing of a musical score.

If the poet works at a regular job, he hasn't got enough time to shake around and keep his ideas in solution. He crystallizes. If he doesn't work at a regular job, he has too much leisure to spend and no money. He gets into debt and bad health, eats on his own soul. It is very much too bad that his working-life includes so little of sedative routine.

I have mentioned the theater as a possible outlet for poetry and as a source of financial intake for the poet. For fifty years the poets and the theater people have been flirting with one another. In the great times of poetry they did more than that, of course; but even still some poet every now and then writes a playable play in verse. In our own day E. E. Cummings, T. S. Eliot, W. H. Auden, and Bert Brecht have held the attention of theater audiences that did not consist of other poets. On the whole, however, your modern poet conceives his art as a solo performance. He despises interpreters and relinquishes with great reluctance the splendid isolation of print. Also, theater people themselves, although less devoted than poets imagine to the vulgar or naturalistic style, are nevertheless a bit suspicious of the modern poet's hermetism. The poet, of course, is suspicious of everything that has to do with money-making. (Poor child, he has rarely made any since Tennyson.) Also, his confirmed egocentricity makes it difficult for him to render character objectively, which it is necessary for him to do if the poetic theater is to be anything more than a morality-play or a cerebral revue.

The musical theater, the opera, he approaches with more good will than he does the spoken theater, though he is not too happy even there about sharing honors with a composer. I realize that the composer usually hogs the show, sometimes deliberately; but still it is not certain that a loyal collaboration with composers and singers would always leave the poet in second place. It most certainly would not if the art of intoned heroic declamation ever got revived. Such a revival would be necessary if tragedy were to become popular again in our ultra-musical age. And the rebirth of a popular taste for tragedy is not at all inconceivable in a world where moral elegance, economic determinism, and personal defeat are about the only aspects under which the interplay between character and social forces can be described convincingly.

Let me sum up by repeating. That music is an island, like Ceylon or Tahiti, or perhaps even more like England, which Bossuet called "the most famous island in the world." That the waters around it are teeming with digestible fish that travel in schools and are known as painters. That swimming around among these at high speed and spouting as they go are prehistoric monsters called poets, who terrify all living things, fish and islanders alike. That these monsters are quite tame, however, in spite of their furious airs, and that since they have no industrial value just now, and since their presence offers no real danger to musical life or to the fishing industry (for they attack only one another), they are allowed to survive and are occasionally given food. Indeed, their evolutions offer a spectacle that is considered by the islanders to be not only picturesque but salutary, instructive, and grand.

CHAPTER FOUR

LIFE AMONG THE NATIVES, or

Musical habits and customs

MUSICAL society consists of musicians who compose and musicians who do not. Those who do not are called "musical artists," "interpreters," executants, or merely "musicians." Those who do compose have all been executants at one time or another. One only learns to create performable works of music by first learning to perform. The longevity of musical works, however, is dependent on their being performable by executants other than the composer. This particular relation between design and execution is peculiar to music.

There is no such thing today as a serious painter who doesn't execute his own canvases. In the great days of Italian painting there was a tradition of workmanship that envisaged and even required the use of apprentice help. Veronese, for example, was a factory of which the large-scale execution and quantity production were only made possible, at that level of excellence, by the existence of such a tradition. The movie studios today produce as they do by means of a not dissimilar organization. Such formulas of collaboration are indispensable whenever a laborious art has to meet a heavy public demand. Even still the "mural" painters use assistants. But without an apprentice system of education, it is not possible to train assistants in a brush technique similar to the master's, or to depend on them for quick comprehension of his wishes. Hence the co-operation is not efficient, and very little important work can be delegated. Art-painting is really a one-man job today.

Poetry too is nowadays a one-man job. It neither derives from declamatory execution nor contemplates its necessity. Poets don't begin life as actors or elocutionists, and certainly actors and elocutionists do not commonly or normally take up poetic composition. Poetry, like prose writing, is not even recited at all for the most part. It is merely printed. Such reading of it as still goes on takes place privately, silently, in the breast; and although many efforts have been made to reinvigorate the art by bringing it out of the library and back to the stage or barrel-house (there is also a certain market for *viva voce* "readings" at women's clubs and on the radio), on the whole your enlightened poetry-fancier still prefers his poetry in a book. There are advantages and disadvantages in the situation, but discussion of them would be academic. The facts are the facts. And one of the cardinal facts about the poetic art today is that declamation is not essential to it.

Music is different from both poetry and painting in this respect. A musical manuscript is not music in the way that a written poem is poetry. It is merely a project for execution. It can correctly be said to consist of "notes" and to require "interpretation." It has about the same relation to real music that an architect's plan has to a real building. It is not a finished product. Auditive execution is the only possible test of its value.

Architects seem to get on perfectly well without having to pass their youth in the building trades. The successful composers of the past (and of the present) have all been musical artists, frequently virtuosos. The celebrated exceptions of Berlioz and Wagner are not exceptions at all. Because Berlioz was master of the difficult Spanish guitar, and Wagner was a thoroughly trained conductor. (He could also play the piano well enough to compose quite difficult music at it, though not well enough to perform that music effectively after it was written.) Star conducting, as we know it, was at least half his invention (Mendelssohn was partly responsible too), and he wrote the first treatise on the subject. He was one of the most competent executants of his century, unbeatable in an opera-pit.

A further special fact about music writing is that it is not only a matter of planning for execution but also of planning for execution by another, practically any other, musician. It may not be better so, but it is so. Interesting and authoritative as the composer's "interpretation" of his own work always is, necessary as it is frequently for the composer, in order to avoid misreading of his intentions, to perform or conduct his own piece the first time or two it is played in public, still a work has no real life of its own till it has been conducted or performed by persons other than the composer. Only in that collaborative form is it ripe and ready to be assimilated by the whole body of music-consumers. It must be translated into sound, amplified, and, yes, interpreted, before it is much good to anybody.

At this point criticism enters. It used to amuse me in Spain that it should take three children to play bull-fight. One plays bull and another plays toreador, while the third stands on the side-lines and cries "holé!" Music is like that. It takes three people to make music properly, one man to write it, another to play it, and a third to criticize it. Anything else is just a rehearsal.

The third man, if he plays his rôle adequately, must

analyze the audition into its two main components. He must separate in his own mind the personal charm or brilliance of the executant from the composer's material and construction. This separation is a critical act. It is necessary to the comprehension of any collaborative art-work.

Criticism of the solitary arts is possible but never necessary. In the collaborative arts it is an indispensable part of the assimilation-process. It is not surprising, therefore, that the criticism of music and of the theater should be vigorously practiced in the daily press, and widely read, and that architectural criticism, which occupies whole magazines to itself, should be exercised by reputable scholars as well as by the most celebrated architects of our time, whereas the daily reporting of painting shows turns out to be almost uniquely just merchants' blurbs and museum advertising. Poetry-reviewing, on account of poetry's small public, is pretty well limited to the advance-guard literary magazines. When verse is covered occasionally for prestige reasons by the daily and weekly press, the reviewing of it is done by definitely minor poets, who fill up their columns with log-rolling and back-biting.

The separateness of design and execution in the collaborative arts is not necessarily to the esthetic disadvantage of these, as the poets like to pretend. It is, on the whole, rather an advantage, I think; but we shall speak of that another time. Music's particular version of that duality, in any case, is what makes composers the kind of men they are. The necessity of being a good executant in order to compose effectively makes their education long and expensive. Of all the professional trainings, music is the most rigid and the most exigent. Even medicine, law, and scholarship, though they often delay a man's entry into married life, do not interfere with his childhood or adolescence.

Music does. No musician ever passes an average or normal infancy, with all that that means of abundant physical exercise and a certain mental passivity. He must work very hard indeed to learn his musical matters and to train his hand, all in addition to his schoolwork and his play-life. I do not think he is necessarily overworked. I think rather that he is just more elaborately educated than his neighbors. But he does have a different life from theirs, an extra life; and he grows up, as I mentioned some time back, to feel different from them on account of it. Sending music students to special public schools like New York's High School of Music and Art or the European municipal conservatories, where musical training is complemented by general studies, does not diminish much the amount of real work to be got through. It merely trains the musician a little more harmoniously and keeps him from feeling inferior to his little friends because of his musical interests. In any case, musical training is long, elaborate, difficult, and intense. Nobody who has had it ever regrets it or forgets it. And it builds up in the heart of every musician a conviction that those who have had it are not only different from everybody else but definitely superior to most and that all musicians together somehow form an idealistic society in the midst of a tawdry world.

For all this idealism and feeling of superiority, there is nevertheless a rift in the society. The executant and the composer are mutually jealous.

The executant musician is a straight craftsman. His life consists of keeping his hand in, and caring for his tools. His relation to the composer is that of any skilled workman in industry to the engineer whose designs he executes. He often makes more money than the composer, and he refuses to be treated like a servant. He is a hard-working man who practices, performs, gives lessons, and travels. He not infrequently possesses a high degree of literary cultivation. He is impressed by composers but handles them firmly and tries to understand their work. His secret ambition is to achieve enough leisure to indulge in musical composition himself. Failing that, to become an orchestral conductor. He doesn't mind teaching but on the whole prefers to play. He doesn't become an habitual pedagogue except under economic pressure, when he can't earn a living by execution. He enjoys excellent health, can't afford to waste time being ill, in fact, and often lives to an advanced age. He pretends to a certain bohemianism, is really a petty bourgeois. His professional solidarity is complete. His trade-unions are terrifyingly powerful and not unenlightened. Economically, humanly, and politically the workman he most resembles is the printer.

The composer is a transmuted executant. He practices execution as little as possible, but he hasn't forgotten a thing. It is his business to know everything there is to know about executants, because he is completely dependent on them for the execution of his work. Executants, being embarrassed by the composer's broader knowledge, try to avoid the composer. Composers, on the other hand, fearing to be cut off from communication with the executant world, are always running after executants and paying them absurd compliments and begging to be allowed to play chamber-music with them, in the hope of picking up some practical hints about instrumental technique. On the whole, composers and their interpreters get on politely but not too well. Composers find executants mean, vain, and petty. Executants find composers vain, petty, and mean. I suspect the executant's potential income level, which is much higher than the composer's, is at the bottom of all this jealousy and high-hatting.

Composers by themselves don't get on too badly either, but they don't like one another really. They are jovial, witty, back-biting. When young they keep up a courteous familiarity with one another's works. After thirty they preserve an equally courteous ignorance of one another's works. Their professional solidarity is nil. Even in the well-organized and very effective European societies for the collection of performing-rights fees, they are likely to let a few semi-racketeers do the work. They grumble no end about how they are robbed by managers, by performers, and by their own protective associations; but they don't do anything to change matters. Politely gregarious but really very little interested in one another, they are without any of that huddling tendency that poets have, without the simple camaraderie of the painters, and with none of that solid fraternalism that is so impressive among the musical executants.

The island of music is laid out in four concentric circles:

¶1. The outer one defines the requirements of Minimum Musicality. These are musical literacy and an ability to play some instrument otherwise than by ear. Singing doesn't count in the literacy test. Basic instrumental skill usually turns out to be piano-playing. There are some exceptions; but roughly speaking, our musical state can be said to consist entirely of fourth-grade pianists.

¶2. The next circle includes everybody who can play any instrument properly. Call this the region of Special Instrumental Skills. It is divided into pie-shaped sections, each representing an instrument. The pianoforte has its special section here just as the other instruments do, and there is a small terrain allotted to singers. The singers who have a right to inhabit the region of Special Skills are more often than not singers who have had operatic experience. Although the pie-shaped sections are pretty well walled off one from another, they are wide open at both ends. There is free access to them from the surrounding suburbs of Minimum Musicality, and through any of them it is possible to pass into the higher circles.

¶3. The third region is Orchestral Conducting. Its altitude and climate are salubrious; the good things of life, including high public honor, abound. The superiority of conducting as a professional status over mere instrumental virtuosity is due to the fact that its practice requires a broader understanding of both technique and style than playing an instrument does. Its practitioners have a happy life, not only on account of the attendant honors and general prosperity, but also because it is technically the easiest specialty in all music. Residence in this region is usually limited, however, to persons who have migrated into it from the region of Special Instrumental Skills. There is no other access normally.

¶4. The inner circle and summit of our mountain-city is Musical Composition. One does not have to go through Orchestral Conducting to get there; one can jump right over from Special Skills. It is a little difficult to get there directly from Minimum Musicality. It is the summit of musicality because extended music-writing requires some understanding of all musical problems. Composers are the superior class in musical society for the simple reason that they know more than anybody else does about music. This superiority is not necessarily reflected in their income-level.

The opera singer is a special form of singer and a special form of musician. He is the only kind of singer, for instance, who has to know something about music, though he doesn't have to know much. He bears the prestige of a great art-form and dresses handsomely for the rôle. His glamour in the nineteenth century was equal to the glamour of conductors and movie-stars today, and he is still not badly paid when he has work.

The way he lives is the way all other executants would like to live; his house is the type-habitation of the Musical Artist. Not plain slummy like the poet's narrow holes, or barn-like and messy like the painter's, the musical artist's house or flat can best be described, I think, as comfortable but crowded. No doubt the model is, unconsciously, a star's dressing-room. It is full of professional souvenirs and objects of daily utility all mixed up together. It resembles at once a junk-shop, a photographer's vestibule, a one-man museum, and a German kitchen. There is always food around. The furniture is luxurious-looking but nondescript. No matter how spacious the rooms, the inhabitants are always too big for them.

Any musician has a tendency to fill up whatever room he is in, but the opera singer is especially permeating. He just naturally acts at all times as if he were singing a solo on a two-hundred-foot stage. His gestures are large and simple; and he moves about a great deal, never looking at anybody else and never addressing a word to anybody privately, but always speaking to the whole room. He has a way of remaining quiet, motionless almost, when not speaking, but alert, like a soloist between cues. He is hard-working, handsome, healthy (though somewhat hypochondriac). When hope is gone he drinks like a fish. Till then he cares for his health and is cheerful. He knows entertaining anecdotes and loves to do imitations of his colleagues. He lives embedded among scores and photographs and seldom moves his residence.

Composers, on the other hand, are always moving. A painter I know calls them "neat little men who live in hotel-rooms." They are frequently unmarried; but unmarried or not, they are super-old-maids about order. The papers on their desks are arranged in exact and equidistant piles. Their clothes are hung up in closets on hangers. Their shirts and ties are out of sight, and their towels are neatly folded. There is no food around. There isn't even much music around. It is all put away on shelves or in trunks. Ink and pencil are in evidence and some very efficient-looking rulers. It looks as if everything were ready for work, but that work hadn't quite yet begun.

Living in hotels and temporary lodgings, and frequently being unmarried, your composer is a great diner-out. Of all the artist-workers, he is the most consistently social. Those painters who live in touch with the world of decorating and mode and fashion are not infrequently snobs, horrid little snobs, for all their camaraderie and democratic ways. The composer is not a snob at all. He is simply a man of the world who dresses well, converses with some brilliance, and has completely charming manners. He is gracious in any house, however humble or grand; and he rarely makes love to the hostess. He eats and drinks everything but is pretty careful about alcohol, as sedentary workers have to be.

He has small illnesses often and gets over them. His diseases of a chronic nature are likely to be seated in the digestive organs. He rarely lives to a great age unless he keeps up his career as an executant. After all, the child who practices an instrument properly usually learns to live on what muscular exercise is involved in musical practice and in the ordinary errands of education. If he continues throughout his adult life some regular instrumental activity, he keeps pretty well and lives to be old. If he gives up that minimum of muscular movement and alternates heavy eating with the introspective and sedentary practice of musical composition, he is likely to crack up in the fifties, no matter how strong his digestive system or his inherited organic constitution.

If he can survive the crack-up, he is good for another twenty years, frequently his finest and most productive. Your aged poet is not as vigorous a poet as your young poet. Your aged painter is tired, and his work is repetitive. The grandest monuments of musical art are not seldom the work of senescence. *Parsifal* was written at seventy, *Falstaff* after eighty. Brahms published his first symphony at forty. Rameau's whole operatic career took place after fifty. Beethoven's last quartets, Bach's *Art of the Fugue,* César Franck's entire remembered repertory, were all composed by men long past their physical prime.

The composer does not have a turbulent life, even in

youth, as artists are commonly supposed to. He is too busy working at his trade. He leads, I should say, the quietest of all the art-lives. Because music study takes time, music writing is laborious, and manuscript-work cannot often be delegated to a secretary. In middle life your composer takes rather elaborate care of his health.

He frequently marries money.

CHAPTER FIVE

LIFE IN THE BIG CITY, or

The civil status of musicians

THE musical executant is an artisan wage-worker. He executes other men's patterns. He is paid by the hour. At least, that is his minimum wage. He has no choice about what pieces he executes unless he is a soloist. A solo artist can choose among various works acceptable to the management those for which he has a special preparation. Even he cannot go far against the management's wishes, because the management has full veto power at all times. Formerly only orchestral musicians belonged to a union. There is now a soloists' union also in the United States, called the American Guild of Musical Artists, an affiliate, like the American Federation of Musicians, of the American Federation of Labor. Both unions are well-organized, rich, and powerful. Both wear the same workman's uniform, which is the formal afternoon or evening dress of the upper classes. This is recognized by some tax-administrations, notably the French, as a workman's uniform, the price of one or two such outfits being deductible from any executant's annual gross income.

The organizing of musical performances is a business like fruit-vending, even though it may, as it does regularly in the case of the municipal opera houses and the privately endowed symphonic ensembles, run a paper deficit and count itself hence a philanthropy. The impresario business has begun recently, both in Europe and in America, to follow the big-business pattern of interlocking directorates and mergers. Ninety-nine per cent, at least, of concert engagements in the United States now take place under the direction either of the Columbia Concerts Corporation, an affiliate of the Columbia Broadcasting Service, or of the N.B.C. Artists' Service, an affiliate of the National Broadcasting Corporation, which in turn is financed by the same sources as the Radio Corporation of America and as Radio-Keith-Orpheum, a cinema-producing-and-exhibiting consortium operating under patents controlled by the General Electric Company.

Music publishing cannot fail to follow this pattern. Already the Associated Music Publishers, Inc., United

States agency for most of the European-owned performing rights (excepting the French, which are collected by Elkan-Vogel, publishers, of Philadelphia, and the English, which are handled rather vaguely by ASCAP, the American Society of Composers, Authors and Publishers), is the property of an electrical combine known as North American Utilities. This latter group bought up the Associated Music Publishers as an economy (since it would permit them to pay the agency fees to themselves) in the business of furnishing to dance-halls and restaurants by wired transmission popular and semi-popular music, practically all of which requires payment of a performing-rights fee.

The composing of music, on the other hand, is a profession like engineering or literary authorship. The individual composer has usually, in consequence, a dual or even a triple status in society. As an executant he is a workman. As a publisher's employee, a concert organizer, or a salaried instructor in a school, he is either a business man or a white-collar proletarian. Teaching, as I shall explain later, cannot possibly be considered a profession.

Composition is a profession, however, just like law and medicine. To be more exact, it is a profession like literature, scholarship, science, and invention, if I may be allowed to group the professions according to their ways of collecting money for professional services. Law, medicine, architecture, and engineering operate on either the salary or the fee-system. Members of the previously named professions, however, derive their emoluments from the commercial exploitation by outsiders of patents, copyrights, and other property rights recognized by law as inherent in original work. Painters and sculptors operate on both systems. A commissioned portrait or decoration is comparable to a surgical operation, to a lawsuit, to the designing of a house or bridge. It is paid for at some price agreed upon in advance. A picture or statue executed privately and sold to the customer in its finished state occasionally gets paid for several times. Most commonly its first sale-price is all the artist ever gets out of it. But there is in France a legal provision by which the creator (and his estate for fifty years after the creator's death) receives a percentage of the profit every time a work of his is resold at an advanced price. Since French picture-dealers keep no books, this royalty fee is really collectible only after a work has been sold twice at public auction. I mention it to show that in France, at least, the creator of plastic art has not only his right of original sale but also a legal right to share in whatever profits are derived by anybody from subsequent commercial exploitation of his work.

Such a right is granted in our western societies only to authors and original designers, rarely to executants. Literary workers collect royalties, I know, on signed translations, these being considered by the Authors' League of America and by the *Société Française des Gens de Lettres* as a form of creative effort. The American Guild of Musical Artists is endeavoring at this moment to establish similar collections on the sale of gramophone records, maintaining with some justice that a signed "interpretation" is a personal work and that the interpreter should receive a share of whatever profit may accrue to the manufacturer.

The translator of any work that is no longer copyright in its original language is likely to collect a full author's-royalty (the minimum is ten per cent of the retail price). The translator of a copyrighted work merely receives either a flat sum, or a part (usually one-fourth) of the author's ten per cent. The same conditions apply to musical "arrangements," though music publishers prefer, whenever possible, to pay a fixed fee for these. Neither ASCAP nor the American Composers' Alliance has yet made a ruling on the subject.

I mention these apparent exceptions in order to make it perfectly clear that even in border-line cases our western societies consider original design as something just a little bit more important than execution. Either it is paid a special fee, or it is granted a share in the profits of exploitation, or both. I do not defend the practice. I define it.

And although in some cases the designer is allowed, and in others obliged, to execute his own designs, his civil status as a creator is different from and superior to that of the ordinary executant workman. The workman may earn more money. The exploiter may be a millionaire. The creator, the designer, however, has special economic rights in capitalist society (in U.S.S.R. too, we understand). Persons enjoying such rights belong to what are called the Professional Classes, just as much as priests and lawyers and doctors do.

They also enjoy certain intellectual rights, commonly spoken of as their Professional Integrity. All professions bear the following marks of their integrity:

¶1. Members of the profession are the final judges on any question involving technique. This is not true in the crafts, where the worker, although he may have a better idea about execution than his director, must nevertheless follow the pattern and employ the material prescribed for him by somebody else. No executant musician, for instance, has the right to perform publicly an altered or reorchestrated version of a piece of music without the composer's consent; and he can be pursued in the courts if he does so. If a surgeon, however, prefers to cut out appendices with a sterilized can-opener, no power in western society can prevent him from doing so, excepting the individual patient's refusal to be operated on at all.

The nurse, who is a craftsman, is subject to the doctor in every technical matter. Told to take a temperature in one way, she can be denied the right to practice again in any first-class hospital if she insists on taking it in some other way. And although her expulsion from organized nursing will be voted on by her peers, her misconduct nevertheless consists in having disobeyed a formal command of the medical man on the case, that is to say, of her professional superior. Armies function in this same way, and so do police-forces. That is why soldiering is not a profession. It is a craft, because in a pinch everybody can be forced to take orders, even about technique, from the political authority. No professional man takes technical orders from anybody.

¶2. The professional groups operate their own educational machinery and are the only persons legally competent to attest its results. Nobody but a group of lawyers or doctors can certify to any state the fitness of a candidate to practice law or medicine. Nobody but the painters' section of the *Académie des Beaux Arts* can appoint other painters to judge the competitions for the *prix de Rome* in painting. Nobody else can even set the problem. Nobody but composers can attest a student's mastery of the classical techniques of musical composition or admit him to membership in any performing-rights society, though there are in America, I admit, a certain number of prize competitions still judged by orchestral conductors and concert managers. I realize also that even trade-unions set their own standards of skill for membership. But these standards have nothing to do with real competence. They go up or down in difficulty according to the ability of the union to provide labor to the market. Some unions, that of the painters, plasterers, and paperhangers, for example, have been known to close their doors to all new membership for a period of time. This is a radical move, purely economic in motivation, that is practically never imitated by the professional bodies, a great liberality toward talent being always their official policy.

¶3. Their professional solidarity is unique and indissoluble. Merchants fight one another into bankruptcy. Workmen can be turned against one another on nationalistic, religious, racial, politico-philosophical, all sorts of partisan grounds. Not so the professional men. They fight their wars in private. They present a united front to the state and to the customers. They even advertise their professional differences a bit, in order to show how busy they are at keeping the tradition pure. Never do they allow controversy to diminish their authority or their receipts. The medical profession is especially pugnacious toward the practitioners of novel therapeutic systems, like osteopathy and chiropractic. If they can ostracize them they do. If not, they invite them to join up. Every profession administers a body of knowledge that is indispensable to society, and it administers that knowledge as a monopoly. Even divinity, the most quarrelsome of the professions, has its solidarity, as witness the constant collaboration, on all sorts of public matters, of the Cardinal Archbishop with the Protestant Episcopal Bishop and the leader of the Reformed Jews in New York City. In every American city the Ministerial Alliance constitutes, in fact, a sort of pooling of religious interests for the mutual benefit of the clergy and for advantages to religion in general.

For pedagogical purposes the professions are usually divided into the liberal, the technical, and the artistic. The first includes medicine, law, science, scholarship, and divinity. The second includes the various branches of engineering. The third is made up of literature, painting, sculpture, and musical composition. Architecture has a tendency in America to get classed with the technical group on account of its association in modern building with the engineering sciences. In Europe it is still considered, however, as one of the Beautiful Arts and is taught in the same academies as painting, sculpture, and engraving. This grouping of the liberal and technical professions versus the Beautiful Arts is embedded in our whole educational system, to the rather considerable neglect of artistic instruction. The distinction is purely a pedagogical one. In real life the professions group themselves otherwise.

Economically considered, they fall into the three groups I mentioned earlier. Law, medicine, architecture, and divinity are the rich group. There are impoverished persons in this group, of course, especially among the clergy. But divinity can and frequently does get very well paid indeed, at least in perquisites; and the time was when religious foundations were rich like states. Some still are. Persons exercising a profession of the rich group live chiefly on the fee, or hold-up, system. They charge what the traffic will bear.

Literature, scholarship, science, and musical composition make up the poor group. Their practitioners are small proprietors who live by leasing their property rights to commercial concerns.

Painting, sculpture, and engineering are the rich-and-poor group. Their members live both ways, sometimes on fees, sometimes on royalties, sometimes, as in the case of engineers, by bartering their future patent rights against a salary. Hence the enormous differences of financial standing among them at any given level of competence.

Professions of this third group are loosely organized

and full of dissension. Politically, their members lean to the extreme right or to the extreme left according to the size of their income and their feeling of security in it.

Professions of the second group are moderately well-organized, and their members are for the most part politically liberal. The poets are an exception in the latter respect, because they have no incomes. They are politically radical, in consequence; at least they all express radical opinions either of a tory or a revolutionary nature.

Professions in the first group are highly and very competently organized. Their memberships are quick to assimilate technical advance. Politically they are conservative. They have a complete strangle-hold on the educational system.

They seized this after the French Revolution. Rather it was offered them by a triumphant bourgeoisie, which wanted to break the power of the clergy over legal studies and of the guilds over craft-training. The latter power was particularly annoying, because the high guild-standards of workmanship and the durability of artisan products were preventing a flooding of the market with shoddy industrial stuff. So the guilds were abolished (on grounds of liberty, equality, and fraternity). Craft-training has never since been as efficient. Everybody is sent to the same public schools now and sold text-books of the Liberal Arts. The entire population is subjected to an enforced elementary education and a certain amount of enforced secondary education, all of which is calculated to prepare a very small number of students for entrance into the professional schools. The "professions" envisaged are four—law, medicine, white-collar engineering and, believe it or not, pedagogy. The crafts, including musical execution, are not much provided for; and the Beautiful Arts are considered from the consumer's and distributor's rather than from the maker's point of view.

Professional preparation for music, painting, and sculpture is excluded from our universities on the ground that they are not Liberal Arts. All that this means is that they cannot be taught by professional pedagogues. They must be taught, like medicine, by practitioners. At present, painting and sculpture are barely taught at all. The conservatories of musical artisanry carry, most of them, a department that is called Theory and that is devoted chiefly to musical analysis. A few colleges and universities try to take musical composition seriously. Harvard and Princeton have small but celebrated faculties. Unfortunately the young people who specialize in music study early are seldom prepared to pass the College Entrance Board examinations, and the students prepared for these are, as a rule, quite unprepared for advanced instruction in music. It is rarely indeed that one of them can even play an instrument properly. Hence the universities themselves are forced to give what elementary instruction the student can take at that advanced age and send him off to Europe to learn to write.

I am not proposing at this point specific alterations in America's education machine, though many are needed if the United States wishes to have its music grown at home. I am pointing out that adequate instruction, public or private, in the Beautiful Arts is rare and expensive, whereas instruction in those subjects whose practitioners have more economic weight in society is less rare and a great deal less expensive.

The medieval schools did not recognize the Beautiful Arts as we define them. They classed all transmissible knowledge as belonging either to the liberal arts or to the crafts. Complete instruction in both was provided for, however, in medieval society. Painting, sculpture, and architecture were considered as crafts. Music (its grammar and composition) was listed among the liberal arts.

Today all these are certainly professions. I do not think it is possible to consider them otherwise or to describe their designers (in so far as these live by their work as designers) as belonging to any social group other than that part of the bourgeoisie known as the Professional Classes. Economically the composer acts just like a literary author. Intellectually he behaves rather like a surgeon. Morally, if I may be allowed that antiquated term to describe the way people think about themselves, he is likely to compare himself to the priest. In any case, he is a professional man. The only difference between him and the lawyer, for example, is the fact that the profession he belongs to is one that doesn't happen to be particularly well paid just now.

CHAPTER SIX

HOW COMPOSERS EAT, or

Who does what to who and who gets paid

IT IS not necessary here to go into the incomes of musical executants. They have engagements or they don't. If they don't, they take pupils. If they can't get pupils they starve. If they get tired of starving they go on relief. Unemployed musicians of high ability and experience are shockingly numerous in America. The development of sound-films and the radio has thrown thousands out of work. The musicians' union has a large relief budget, however, and the W.P.A. has given musical work to many. Eventually their situation is that of all artisan wage-workers in crowded crafts. Their large numbers and their powerful union organization have made it advisable to handle the problem of large-scale indigence among them by means of a definite social policy. This policy is operated in part directly by the union itself (plus some free-lance philanthropic organizations like the Musicians' Emergency Relief Committee) and partly by the Federal Government, though government action is not taken, of course, entirely without pressure from the union.

Composers, being professional men and not too well organized at that, have not yet found themselves the object of public concern. They do have, however, their little financial problems, I assure you, not the least of which is bare existence.

The poet of thirty works, whenever that is possible, at something not connected with literature. The composer practically always works at music, unless he can manage to get himself kept. He plays in cafés and concerts. He conducts. He writes criticism. He sings in church choirs. He reads manuscripts for music publishers. He acts as music librarian to institutions. He becomes a professor. He writes books. He lectures on the Appreciation of Music. Very occasionally he holds down a job that is in no way connected with music.

A surprisingly large number of composers are men of private fortune. Some of these have it from papa, but the number of those who have married their money is not small. The composer, in fact, is rather in demand as a husband. Boston and New England generally are noted for the high position there allotted to musicians in the social hierarchy and for the number of gifted composers who have in consequence married into flowery beds of ease. I don't know why so many composers marry well, but they do. It is a fact. I don't suppose their sexuality is any more impressive than anybody else's, though certainly, as intellectuals go, the musician yields to none in that domain. After all, if a lady of means really wants an artistic husband, a composer is about the best bet, I imagine. Painters are notoriously unfaithful, and they don't age gracefully. They dry up and sour. Sculptors are of an incredible stupidity. Poets are either too violent or too tame, and terrifyingly expensive. Also, due to the exhausting nature of their early lives, they are likely to be impotent after forty. Pianists and singers are megalomaniacs; conductors worse. Besides, executants don't stay home enough. The composer, of all the art-workers in the vineyard, has the prettiest manners and ripens the most satisfactorily. His intellectual and his amorous powers seldom give completely out before death. His musical powers not uncommonly increase. Anyway, lots of composers marry money, and a few have it already from papa. Private fortune is a perfectly good source of income for musicians. It is not as difficult for a rich man to write music as it is for him to write poetry. The class censorship is not so strict. The only trouble about money for composers is that spending it takes time. The musician who runs all over town giving lessons and playing accompaniments has often just as much leisure to write music as does the ornamental husband of a well-to-do lady living in five elegant houses.

Many composers are able to live for years on gifts and doles. Include among these all prizes and private commissions. I don't suppose anybody believes nowadays that money one has earned is any more ennobling than money one hasn't. Money is money, and its lack of odor has often been remarked. Gifts sometimes have strings, of course; but so has any job its inconveniences. Equally punctured, I take it, is the superstition formerly current that struggle and poverty are good for the artist, who is a lazy man and who only works when destitute. Quite the contrary, I assure you. Composers work better and faster when they have a bit of bourgeois comfort. Too much money, with its attendant obligations, is a nuisance to any busy man. But poverty, illness, hunger, and cold never did any good to anybody. And don't let anyone tell you differently.

The number of composers who live on the receipts from their compositions is very small, even in Europe, though on both of the northwestern continents that number is larger in the field of light music than it is in the domain of massive instrumentation and extended length. We owe indeed to the composers of light music that we are able to get paid at all for our performing rights, since it is they who have always organized the societies for exacting such payment and furnished the money for fighting infringers in the courts.

Royalties and performing-rights fees are to any composer a sweetly solemn thought. They are comparatively rare, however, in America, since composers, even composers of popular music, are nothing like as powerfully organized there for collecting them as the electrical and banking interests (whose shadow darkens our prospects of profit in all musical usages) are for preventing their being collected. So that when every now and then some composer actually makes enough money off his music to sleep and eat for a while, that is a gala day for the musical art. He feels like a birthday-child, of course, and fancies himself no end. Let him. His distinction carries no security. And he had better keep his hand in at performing and teaching and writing and at all the other little ways he knows of turning a not too dishonest extra penny. He had better seize on the first flush of fame too to "guest-conduct" his own works. This brings in two fees at once, one for his conducting and one for his performing rights. Invariably the composer who has enough composer-income to live on can pick up quite decent supplementary sums, as well as keep his contacts fresh, by not giving up entirely traffic in the by-products of his musical education.

I have been running on in this wandering fashion because I wanted to show how flexible is the composer's economic life and how many strings he has to his bow. Briefly, the composer's possible income-sources are:

¶1. Non-musical jobs, or earned income from non-musical sources.

¶2. Unearned income from all sources.

- [a.] Money from home
  - (x.) His own
  - (y.) His wife's
- [b.] Other people's money
  - (x.) Patronage
    - i. Subventions
    - ii. Commissions
  - (y.) Prizes
  - (z.) Doles

¶3. Other men's music, or selling the by-products of his musical education.

- [a.] Execution
- [b.] Organizing musical performances
- [c.] Publishing and editing
- [d.] Pedagogy
- [e.] Lecturing

[f.] Criticism and musical journalism

[g.] The Appreciation-racket

¶4. The just rewards of his labor.

[a.] Royalties

(x.) From music published

(y.) From gramophone-recordings

[b.] Performing-rights fees.

Every composer receives the money he lives on from one of these sources. Most have received money from several. I have lived on nearly all of them at one time or another.

Between the extremes of being too rich for comfort and being really poor, the amount of money composers have doesn't seem to affect them very much. Photogenic poverty and ostentatious spending are equally repugnant to their habits. The source of their money has, however, a certain effect on their work. We have noted that the composer, being a member of the Professional Classes, enjoys all the rights and is subject to the obligations of what is known as Professional Integrity. This does not mean that he enjoys complete intellectual freedom. He has that only with regard to the formal, or structural, aspects of his art. His musical material and style would seem to be a function, at any given moment, of his chief income-source.

CHAPTER SEVEN

WHY COMPOSERS WRITE HOW, or

The economic determinism of musical style

BEFORE I go on to explain how a composer's chief income-source affects his musical style, I think I had better say what is ordinarily meant by style in music. It is not the same thing as style in literature, for instance, which is mostly considered nowadays to be personal. The word style is employed in four ways with regard to music.

Its most precise usage is a technical one. The phrases "fugal style," "canonic style," "modal style," and the like are all descriptions of syntactic devices. They are methods of achieving coherence. More recent devices of similar nature are the "chromatic" style, the "atonal" style, the "dissonant tonal" style, even the "jazz" or "swing" style. These last two refer, of course, to rhythmic texture within a given tonal syntax; but the rhythmic texture of swing is just as much a technical device for achieving coherence as the twelve-tone system of atonality is.

The ensemble of technical procedures plus personal mannerisms that marks the work of any given composer or period of composition is also referred to as the style of that composer or period. One can say that a piece is written in the style of Schumann or in the style of Handel or in the style of Debussy. Writing "in the style of" is taught at some music schools. It is used in musical practice chiefly for the "faking" (improvisation from a figured bass) of harpsichord accompaniments to pre-nineteenth-century music and for the composition of Roman Catholic masses, the "style of Palestrina" having been firmly recommended to modern composers by the papal Bull of 1911 known as *De Motu Proprio.*

Pianistic, violinistic, vocal, and similar adjectives, when they qualify the word "style," indicate a manner of writing that is convenient to the instruments so referred to, that is "grateful" to execute upon them, or that suggests their characteristics.

The word is used sometimes also in a qualitative sense. An artist is said to perform with "good" or "bad" style. A piece may not be said to be written in good or bad style, but if it is well written it may be said to have "style."

For the present discussion I shall try to limit the word to its first associations, to the divers syntactic devices that are available to any composer. This is the commonest usage of the word as applicable to musical composition. A composer's choice among these devices I shall call his stylistic orientation. It will not be necessary, I think, to employ the executional and qualitative meanings at all. It will be necessary, however, to distinguish between style and subject-matter.

The subject-matter of vocal music is its verbal text. The subject-matter of theater-music is whatever the stage-directions say it is. The subject-matter of an instrumental concert piece is not necessarily what the composer says it is. If he calls it *The Rustle of Spring* or *Also Sprach Zarathustra,* we can take him at his word. But if he calls it *Fifth Nocturne* or *Symphony in F,* we can never be sure. Sometimes it is an objective piece that was written to illustrate some program that he isn't telling us, and sometimes it is a depiction of non-verbalized visceral feelings. In the latter case, the subject-matter is pretty hard to describe verbally. "Absolute" was the nineteenth-century term the Germans used for such music. That meant that no matter how the composer wrote it or what he was thinking about, the piece could be satisfactorily enjoyed without verbal aids. The term "absolute" being now superannuated, I propose to substitute "introspective"; and I think we can apply it as "absolute" was applied, to all music that has no verbal text, no specific usage, and no evocative title.

Let us now return to the four sources of income and examine their relation to the composer's work in general and to his stylistic orientation in particular.

¶1. *Non-Musical Jobs,* or *Earned Income from Non-Musical Sources.*

The composer who lives by non-musical work is rare; but still there are some. The chief mark of his work is its absence of professionalism. It is essentially naïve. It breaks through professional categories, despises professional conventions. The familiarity with instrumental limitations and current interpretative traditions that composers have who are constantly working with the executant world is of great practical advantage in most respects. Your naïve composer has no such mastery of well-known methods, no such traditional esthetic. The professional makes esthetic advance slowly, if at all, progressing step by step, in touch at all times with the music world. The naïf makes up his music out of whole cloth at home. He invents his own esthetic. When his work turns out to be not unplayable technically, it often gives a useful kick in the pants to the professional tradition.

The music of Moussorgsky, of Erik Satie, and of the American Charles Ives did that very vigorously indeed.

The naïfs show no common tendency in stylistic orientation. Their repertory of syntactical device is limited to what they can imitate plus what they make up for themselves. They are like children playing alone. Their subject-matter is likely to be the great literary classics, their comprehension of these atavistic and profoundly racial. They put Dante to music, and Shakespere, Dialogues of Plato, the Book of Revelation. They interpret these in terms of familiar folklore, remembered classics, and street-noises. They derive their melodic material from hymns and canticles, from jazzways and darn-fool ditties. They quote when they feel like it. They misquote if they prefer. They have none of the professional's prejudices about "noble" material or stylistic unity. They make music the way they like it, for fun. The naïfs are rare whose technique is ample enough to enable them to compete at all with Big Time. They mostly flower unknown and unheard. Those whom we do encounter are angels of refreshment and light, and their music is no small scandal. Its clarity is a shock to the professional mind. It doesn't hesitate about being lengthy or about being brief, and it neglects completely to calculate audience-psychology. It is not made for audiences. As Tristan Tzara said of Dada, it is a "private bell for inexplicable needs." It is beyond mode and fashion. It is completely personal and gratuitous.

¶2. *Unearned Income from All Sources.*

[a.] *Money from home*

(x.) *His own*

The composer whose chief revenue comes from invested capital shows the following marks of his economic class:

His subject-matter reflects the preoccupations of his kind. In the present age it reflects that avoidance of serious remarks that is practiced in capitalist circles today. He tends to write playful music, to seek charm at the expense of emphasis. He abounds in witty ingenuities. He is not given much just now to writing introspective music. Before the war, when refined Europeans with incomes gave up most of their time to introspection, both sentimental and analytic, the financially independent composer wrote a great many symphonies and reveries. Ernest Chausson and Albéric Magnard should serve to fix the pre-war type for us. Francis Poulenc will do for the European post-war capitalists. In America there is John Alden Carpenter.

The stylistic orientation of the rich composer is toward

the French salon-school. He goes in for imagistic evocation, witty juxtapositions, imprecise melodic contours, delicacy of harmonic texture and of instrumentation, meditative sensuality, tenderness about children, evanescence, the light touch, discontinuity, elegance. Debussy is his ideal and model, though Debussy himself was not financially independent till after his second marriage.

(y.) *His wife's*

The composers who have married their incomes are not so likely to be Debussyans as they were twenty years ago. If they marry money too young they don't get much time to write music anyway. They are put through the paces of upper-class life pretty much all day long. If they marry their money in middle life, their working habits are already formed. Also their stylistic orientation. Sometimes nothing changes at all, especially if there isn't too much money around. If there is a lot of money, class pressure is pretty strong. The composer subjected to it is likely to turn toward capitalistic proletarianism. There are two common forms of this. One is the exploitation of ornamental folklore (somebody else's folklore). The other is a cult of urban populistic theatrical jazz (jazz by evocation) and of pseudo-Viennese waltzes.

The relation of music writing to unearned income is about like this. Unquestionably children get the best preparation for professional life in families that are well enough off to have access to first-class instruction. In families where there is big money around, the children are always kept so busy learning how to live like rich people that serious musical instruction is usually out of the question. The families of professional men and of prosperous shop-keepers continue to supply the bulk of talent to the artistic professions. The musician rarely inherits from such a family enough to live on once he is grown and educated. In richer families he seldom learns much music. When he does, or when, having mastered his art in less disturbing circumstances, he insures his future income by marriage, there is nothing to prevent his achieving the highest distinction as a composer. He does, however, tend to write the kind of music I describe.

The sources of contributory income are without effect on the gentleman composer (or on any other for that matter), unless they provide what would be enough money to live on if he were not independent, and unless, of course, the professional experience entailed may give him a bias toward the pianoforte or the violin or some other instrument. He has class bias about both subject-matter and style, but he does not have any of the occupational conditionings of the musical journalist, of the pedagogue, or of the executant concert artist.

[b.] *Other people's money*

Let us take for granted that every professional composer has had access by one means and another to adequate instruction. It is necessary to assume this, because if he hasn't by the age of twenty-five come into contact with all the chief techniques, he must count as a naïve composer. The naïfs, like the composers of popular music, can achieve high distinction; but their music is never influenced by the source of the money they live on. If it were, they would not be naïve. Naïfs exist in all classes of society. Professional musicians are mostly bourgeois and mostly petty bourgeois.

It is not certain that this is the necessary class situation of the composer, as we have just seen. It is simply that the rich are mostly too busy and the poor too poor to get educated in musical technique. Musical instruction is so expensive, even in slum music schools, that only the bourgeoisie has complete access to it; and only those families who live in the more modest economic levels of the bourgeoisie have sufficient leisure to oversee a proper musical upbringing. This is why, although there is some ruling-class art-music, there is no proletarian art-music at all except what is written at the proletariat from above. The poor farmer and the mountaineer, the slum child and the segregated negro, have open to them only the simple popular ways, the folk-ways. They make beautiful music, very beautiful music indeed. Jazz, swing, hodowns, chanties, hymn-lore from the Southern uplands, work-songs, dance-ditties, cowboys' laments, fiddle-jigs, torch songs, blues, ballads from the barrack-room and barrel-house, children's games, prison wails, collegiate comics, sentimental love-songs, waltzes, tangos, fox-trots, and the syncopated Scotch-African spirituals—nine-tenths of all these are made up and brought to their definitive shape by poor people. It isn't vigor or musical understanding or inspiration that the poor lack. They have everything for making music but access to the written tradition. Massive instrumentation and the structural devices that make possible the writing of long pieces are the property of the trained musician, and he comes mostly from the lower economic levels of the bourgeoisie. Again I do not defend or deplore. At least not in this book. I am here occupied in describing the state of the musical tradition in Western society and in telling how it actually works.

(x.) *Patronage*

Let us now tell, therefore, how a composer (we have already got him educated) gets hold of money to live on when he hasn't a rich papa or wife. It is extraordinary the amounts of money, just plain gift money, that a composer with some social charm (and they all have that) can put his fingers on, especially in early manhood. Some go on getting it till they die.

There seem to be two formulas for giving money to composers. One is direct subvention. The other is the commissioning of works. The latter is really a kind of subvention, because the ordering of musical works nowadays is practically never an expression of the patron's musical needs. Half the time he doesn't even have the work performed once it is delivered. In the cases when he does, there is always an air of inexpensive philanthropy around, and a careful disclaiming of any responsibility on the patron's part for the nature and content of the piece. The piece is usually an orchestral or chamber-work called *Symphony* or *Sonata* or something equally non-committal.

i. *Subvention*

Composers who live on straight subvention tend to write introspective music of violent harmonic texture and picturesque instrumental style. They write very long pieces. They are not much bothered about charm, elegance, sentiment, or comprehensibility, though they are seldom deliberately hermetic. They go in for high-flown lyricism and dynamic punch, seldom for contrapuntal texture, unless that seems to heighten lyrical expressiveness. They are revolters against convention. At least, that is their pose. Beethoven is their ideal; and they think of themselves as prophets in a wilderness, as martyrs unappreciated, as persecuted men. The trick of appearing to be persecuted is, of course, their way of earning their living. The minute they lose that air of being brave men downed by circumstances, they cease to get any money. Because tender-hearted people with money to give away don't like giving it to serene or successful characters, no matter how poor the latter may be. When a composer who has been living for some years on patronage and gifts starts earning his own money, there is always a noticeable change in his music. His subject-matter becomes less egocentric. His musical style becomes less violently picturesque and a good deal easier to follow. He eventually stops over-writing the brass in his orchestral scores.

ii. *Commissions*

Composers are rare who can pull down commissions all their lives. But my theories about economic determinism do not demand that the composer live from any given source for a long time before his music begins to reflect that source. On the contrary, I maintain that composers vary their manner from piece to piece in direct conformity with their income-source of the moment, the subject-matter and the stylistic orientation of any musical work being largely determined by the source of the money the composer is living on while writing that piece.

Privately commissioned works, therefore, should show some kind of uniformity. Which they do. Less Beethovenesque than the works of the steadily subventioned, less violent, and less animated by personal dynamism, they lean toward an abstract style. I am not even certain that the international neo-classic style was not worked out as a stylistic medium for privately commissioned works, as a sort of *lingua franca* that could be addressed to any possible patroness anywhere in the Western world. During the 1920's there were just about enough available patronesses in America, France, Belgium, Germany, England, Switzerland, and Hungary, all put together, to enable a clever composer to get hold of with luck about one of these commissions a year. This gave him a basic income of from one to two thousand dollars.

What is the international style for privately commissioned works? It is a dissonant contrapuntal manner welded out of the following heterogeneous elements, all chosen for their prestige value:

A. The animated contrapuntalism of J. S. Bach,

B. The unresolved dissonances of Debussy and Richard Strauss, and

C. The Berlioz tradition of instrumentation.

[This is the instrumentation of Berlioz, Bizet,

Saint-Saëns, Rimsky-Korsakov, Chabrier, Debussy, Ravel, and Stravinsky. It is differential instrumentation. Clarity and brilliance are achieved by keeping the different instruments at all times recognizably separate. A thin and reed-like fiddle tone is presupposed.

[The rival tradition is that of Meyerbeer, Wagner, Brahms, Tchaikovsky, Mahler, Strauss, Schoenberg, and Puccini. This is absorptive instrumentation. Emotional power and tonal weight are achieved by lots of doubling at the unison, which is to say by the building up of composite instrumental timbres, all sounding somewhat alike but differing greatly in weight and carrying power. It presupposes a husky and vibrant fiddle tone. The German tradition is a perfectly good one, as you can see from the big names connected with it. It has not enjoyed the same international prestige, however, since the World War, as the Franco-Russian.]

D. To these elements were added frequently a fourth, the reconstructed or modern French sonata-form—a device practiced originally by the pupils of César Franck and expounded at Vincent d'Indy's Schola Cantorum.

The sonata-form was invented in Vienna by K. P. E.

Bach, and it flourished there as the pet continuity device of Haydn, Mozart, Beethoven, Schubert, Schumann, Brahms, and Mahler. It was introduced into France by Reyer in 1845, practiced and fought for by Camille Saint-Saëns, and finally domesticated by César Franck. Since the death of Johannes Brahms it has been very little practiced in Vienna. What is practiced today in Paris (and internationally) is not the Viennese sonata-form at all. It is a French reconstruction for pedagogical purposes. D'Indy is largely its inventor. It is based on certain practices of Haydn and Beethoven. It has not yet been successfully introduced into Vienna. It enjoys world-wide prestige, however, a prestige borrowed from that of the Viennese masters and based on the extreme simplicity of the reconstruction, all of which makes it just fine for pedagogy and for international prize-winning. The Viennese form, when it was alive, was never very teachable outside of Vienna, because no two examples of it were ever near enough alike to make standardization possible. The good ones all seem to be exceptions to some rule of which nobody has ever seen a typical case in point.

The French orchestral palette presents no especial difficulties. Any good student can handle it. And the writing of animated counterpoint in the dissonant style is easy as falling off a log. The real difficulty about any contrapuntal style is length and always has been. Now the modern-music fan likes his pieces fairly long. Nothing under twenty minutes will impress him very much. And twenty minutes of wiggly counterpoint are too much (because too vague) for anybody. Bach had the same problem to face. Fugal construction helped him over many a bad moment. But modern audiences won't listen to fugues very long or very often. They lack punch. Sonata-form, even in its rather static reconstructed version, is about the only dependable device (outside of literary texts and verbal programs) that will enable a composer to give continuity to a long and varied movement.

It offers free play to sustained lyricism, to stormy drama, and to emphatic orchestration. But these are two musical styles it cannot digest very well, the animated contrapuntal and the strictly dissonant. The first is inimical to it because that kind of counterpoint, whether practiced in a Brandenburg concerto or in an improvised swing session, being a cerebral manifestation, viscerally static. And sonata-form is only good for dramatizing visceral states, which are never static, which, quite to the contrary, are constantly varying in intensity, constantly moving about over the pleasure-pain and the tranquillity-anxiety scales. Systematic dissonance is inimical to the essential virtues of sonata-form for a similar reason, those virtues being all of a dramatic nature. The sonata is abstract musical theater, a dramatization of non-verbalized emotions. There is no sonata without drama, struggle, the interplay of tensions. Systematic dissonance, like systematic consonance, is the contrary of any such interplay. It too is viscerally static.

For the bright young composers of the world, who knew all this long ago, to have gone in as thoroughly as they did, between the years of 1920 and 1935, for such an indigestible mixture, such a cocktail of culture as the international neo-classic style, leaves us no out but to ascribe to them a strong non-musical motivation. The sharing of the available private commissions of the Western world among a smallish but well-united group of these composers I maintain to have been the motivation. That and the corollary activities of winning prizes and foundational awards and eventually, when all the prizes and all the possible commissions have been had, of grabbing off one of the fancier institutional teaching jobs.

Because the international style is God's gift to pedagogy. That we shall go into in another place, perhaps. Here just let me mention the slight but interesting differences of style possible within the internationalist conception.

For private commissions, a long piece is indicated in dissonant contrapuntal style, neutral in emotional content and hermetic in expression. It should be a bit difficult to listen to and very difficult to comprehend, yet withal skillful enough in instrumentation that nobody could call the work incompetent. A maximum of impressiveness and a minimum of direct significance are the desiderata.

(y.) *Prizes*

For foundational awards and prize-competitions the above strict formula needs a little alleviation. Sometimes the injection of a lush sentimental tune here and there will satisfy the judges of the candidate's fitness for eventually pleasing a large public. More respectable, however, is the substitution of some picturesque folklore or other for original melodic material. Folklore, as you can easily see, adds popular charm without the loss of cultural prestige. A nice dosage of dissonance proves the candidate's modernism. A bit of counterpoint will show his good will toward pedagogy. And brilliant orchestration guarantees musicianship. Prize committees, mark you, never judge musical mastery on anything but orchestration. They can't. Because counterpoint is too easy to write; anyone can do it; everything sounds well enough; no judgment of its merits is possible. And harmony is difficult to judge; the gulf is of but a hairsbreadth between superb and lousy. Melodic material, tunes, can only be judged by the way they stand up under usage. Formalized construction is not one of the essential elements of music, but that too can only be judged from usage. Instrumentation is the one element of musical composition that is capable of being judged objectively today, because it is the one element that is taught, learned, and practiced according to a tradition that has been unbroken for the past hundred years, and that is accepted intact, especially the French version of it, by all educated musicians.

The international-style music world used to be a well-organized going concern, with its own magazines, its "contemporary music" societies, its subventions, its conspiracies, and its festivals. Of late years business has not been so good. Private commissions are scarce, institutional funds diminished, the societies defunct or moribund, the public fed-up. The high-pressure salesmanship that forced into the big orchestral concerts (by pretending that an international movement should be supported on nationalistic grounds) music that was never intended for anything but prize-winning and the impressing of other musicians, has given a black eye to all music written since 1918. The general music public and the trustee class have both revolted. The conductors have seized the occasion to pull all the cover over to their side of the bed, thus leaving quite out in the cold the problem of contemporary composition in large form (which presupposes as an essential factor in the equation the presence of a large general public). I know there still appear new pieces periodically on the orchestral programs, though less frequently than before 1932, the year in which the trustees of the Philadelphia Symphony Society formally warned Leopold Stokowski to lay off modern music. Everywhere the preceding decade's chief offender (the international style) is taboo. Boston is an exception in this, because one of the movement's chief survivors, Walter Piston, is head of the Department of Music at Harvard; and his works must of course be performed. The new pieces most orchestras play nowadays are in the vein of pre-war post-Romanticism. They are chiefly by school-teachers and children just out of the conservatories. They are often tuneful and pleasing. They seldom get a second performance, however, even when the first goes over big, as it does not infrequently. I don't think the conductors quite want any composer to have a very steady public success. They consider success their domain. And their success depends on keeping orchestral performance a luxury product, a miraculously smooth, fabulously expensive, and quite unnecessary frame for sure-fire classics.

(z.) *Doles*

A special category of patronage is the government dole. When home-relief is a composer's chief source of income, he isn't likely to write music at all. Life is too difficult, too desolate. When, as in Europe, it is less than minimum sustenance, he tends to become proletarian class-conscious, to tie up with a Marxian party (usually the Communist), and to produce angry music of exaggerated simplicity and a certain deliberate vulgarity.

The W.P.A., America's work-relief organization, never had a Composers' Project. A number of composers were engaged, however, to write music for theatrical productions; and quite a few more were placed on the regular Music Project as executants. The W.P.A. theater people did quite well by music. They showed as good taste in their choice of composers as they did in their choice of plays and directors. The Federal Theater was for the years 1935 and 1936 the most vigorous new art movement in the whole West. The music written for its productions varied greatly in style and subject-matter, as all music must that is ordered and paid for with a specific art purpose in view. The composers who wrote music for the Federal Theater are not classifiable as dole-subjects or charity-cases. They were earning their living by musical composition, and their music bears all the marks of music that has paid its way.

¶3. *Other Men's Music,* or *Selling the By-Products of His Musical Education.*

[a.] *Execution*

People who earn their bread by playing the piano or playing the organ or playing the violin or conducting, by musical interpretation in short, are the most timid of all when they start writing music. They have only one idea in their heads and that is to write "gratefully" for the instrument in question. They often succeed in doing so. Their subject-matter is likely to be pale, wan, and derivative.

This was not always so. Exploring the musical possibilities of any new instrument or medium is a job for persons who play that instrument. The history of violin-composition in the seventeenth century, of writing for the harpsichord and for the organ clear up to the death of J. S. Bach, of piano music in the nineteenth century, of swing music in our own, is the history of performing virtuosos who composed. From the time of Corelli and Domenico Scarlatti to Chopin and Franz Liszt, all the solo instruments were the springboards of musical art; and many of the greatest masters of musical composition earned their living by instrumental virtuosity, even by the interpretation of other men's work. Richard Wagner was about the last of the great interpreter-composers in the non-popular tradition.

Today all composers can play an instrument still, and most can conduct if they have to, but they avoid doing either steadily. Instrumental virtuosity and the interpretation of "classical" music have both reached the point of diminishing artistic returns to the composer. The expansion of techniques has so slowed down that regular practice is no longer a source of constant revelation to him. Rather it stupefies his imagination and limits his musical horizon.

This is not true in the swing-world, where technique is still expanding. Duke Ellington is a number-one swing-pianist and a number-one swing-composer. The music of Ignaz Paderewski, of Ferruccio Busoni, of Charles-Marie Widor, and of Fritz Kreisler (even including his clever fakings of early violin-writers) cannot possibly be considered to be anything like so high-class as their respective instrumental performances.

A bit of concert work is good for composers in their youth. The organ and the kettledrums seem to be especially useful for amplifying the musical conceptions of people brought up on the pianoforte or the violin. The first introduces them to quantitative meter. The second sharpens their sense of pitch. Both are invaluable trainings in rhythmic exactitude and in notation.

[b. and c.] *Organizing, publishing, and editing*

The organizing of concerts and the publishing business are both bad for composition. They are businesses, not crafts. They contribute nothing to a composer's musical experience. The composers who get involved with them write music less and less. Arranging and editing are all right. The trouble with them is that they don't pay enough. It is rare that a composer can exist on their proceeds for any length of time. They are best done by performers and conductors as a side-line.

[d.] *Pedagogy*

I sometimes think the worst mischief a composer can get into is teaching. I mean as a main source of income. As a supplementary source a little of it doesn't hurt, is rather good, in fact, for clarifying and refreshing the mind. A little criticism or musical journalism is good too. A lot of either is not so good, because they both get you worried about other men's music. Whenever the by-products of his musical education become for any length of time the main source of a composer's income, occupational diseases and deformities set in.

As everybody knows, school-teachers tend to be bossy, pompous, vain, opinionated, and hard-boiled. This is merely their front, their advertising. Inside they are timid and over-scrupulous. Their music, in consequence, comes out looking obscure and complex. Its subject-matter, its musical material are likely to be over-subtle and dilute. When we say nowadays that a work is "academic" we mean all that and more. We mean that the means employed are elaborate out of all proportion to the end achieved.

When I speak of pedagogues I mean teachers who live by their teaching, whether they teach privately or in institutions. All teachers who live by teaching are alike. The holders of sinecure posts (sadly lacking in the United States) are an exception. The director of any French conservatory, for instance, is always an elderly composer of distinction. He is not expected to do anything but an overseer's job, to protect, from the vantage point of his years and experience, the preservation intact, with all necessary renewals, whatever tradition of musical instruction that institution represents. He is not expected to bother with administrative detail or to drum up trade for his institution or to have anything whatsoever to do with trustees. He may dine occasionally with the Minister of Public Instruction and the Secretary for the Fine Arts. An hour a day will cover all his duties. His job lasts till he dies, short of public moral turpitude on his part. A smaller sinecure sometimes available to young composers is the librarianship of a conservatory. The absence of sinecures in the United States is one-half the trouble with music-teaching. It is impossible to get a twelve-hundred-dollar-a-year music job at any college I know of that doesn't end by taking about fifty hours a week to accomplish and to keep. The other half is what is the matter with music-teaching anywhere, with living off any of what I have called the by-products of a musical education. It is the constant association with dead men's music that they entail. Only in vacation time, if there is any money left to take a vacation, does the school-teacher get a chance to forget all that, to put the classics out of reach at the bottom of his mind, well out of the way of the creative act. Daily dealing with the music of the past is probably all right after fifty. It never fails to produce in a younger man a derivative manner of writing that no amount of surface-complexity can conceal.

Teachers tend to form opinions about music, and these are always getting in the way of creation. The teacher, like the parent, must always have an answer for everything. If he doesn't he loses prestige. He must make up a story about music and stick to it. Nothing is more sterilizing. Because no one can make any statement three times without starting to believe it himself. One ends by being full of definite ideas about music; and one's mind, which for creative purposes should remain as vague and unprejudiced as possible, is corseted with opinions and *partis pris*. Not the least dangerous of these *partis pris* is the assumption that since the finest examples of musical skill and stylization from the past (the so-called "classics") are the best models to expose before the young, they are necessarily the best models for a mature composer to follow in his work. This is very nearly the opposite of the real truth. As Juan Gris used to say about painting, "the way to become a classic is by not resembling the classics in any way."

When I speak of teaching, I mean teaching for money; and I deplore it, for composers, as a habit-forming vice. I would not wish, however, that the young composer be denied access to professional advice. He is, in fact, not denied it. Professional composers are only too delighted to read over the works of the young and to give practical advice where needed. They enjoy the homage implied; they like the chance to steal a good trick; they like seeing their own tricks stolen and advertised. All this can take place without any exchange of money. It is free graduate-instruction. Elementary instruction (which is a bore to give) must always be paid for, and usually the student gets his best money's worth from regular pedagogues who are not composers.

Allow me, please, at this point to digress a little further on the subject of how people learn to write music. You never learn anything technical except from somebody who possesses technique. You can only learn singing from a singer, piano-playing from a pianist, conducting from a conductor; and you can only master so much of these techniques as the instructor himself has mastered. There are, however, elementary subjects which are so conventional that their mastery requires no personalized skill and implies no higher achievement. It is not necessary, for example, or even very desirable to try to learn grammar from a poet. Any school-teacher is better, can show you better how to parse, decline, and diagram according to accepted convention. So with solfeggio, counterpoint, fugue. They are stylized drills, not living skills. Harmony is the difficult branch to learn, because it is neither really stylized nor really free. I doubt if anybody can teach it satisfactorily; but even still a routine pedagogue is usually quicker and more effective about it than a composer is. Orchestration is different. It can only be learned from a composer or from a professional orchestrator. The subject is a completely practical one and requires a practical man. All the text-books are by practical men like Berlioz and Strauss and Rimsky-Korsakov and Widor. Musical form is also a practical matter. It is scarcely a subject at all and can only be advised about after the fact. There is no text-book on the subject, no formal instruction available.

How then can musical education be organized so that the instructor's as well as the student's interest may be respected? Singing and playing must be taught, as they are now, by singers and players or by ex-singers and ex-players. The elements of musical theory (that is to say harmony, counterpoint, fugue, and musical analysis) should be taught, as they are not always now, by trained seals, which is to say by persons especially prepared for that drill-work, by pure pedagogues. Instrumentation must be taught by composers; there is no way around it. But since the composer is not much benefited musically by teaching, some arrangement must be reached that will serve his interests as well as the student's. One of the best is to use as professors of instrumentation only men over fifty. These can teach an hour a day something they know without getting vicious about it. Also, the whole system of musical instruction must be co-ordinated and watched over by a composer, an elderly one preferably, and one for whom the job is either a sinecure or else a quite negligible source of income. It should never be full-time work.

As for the actual composition of music in the early stages of a student's career, he had better keep that as separate as possible from his life as a student. Let him show his efforts to other composers, to friends, to anybody but to his professors. Unless the teacher in question is or has been a successful composer, the student will only get confusion and discouragement out of him.

[e. and f.] *Lecturing, criticism, and musical journalism*

Turning an odd penny here and there by lecturing doesn't count. Earning one's bread by lecturing does. But lecturing is not a trade in itself; it is always something else. Either it is teaching, or it is criticism, or it is the Appreciation-racket, or it is musical interpretation. Sometimes it is all four. I mention it separately, merely because it is a common way of earning money.

Criticism and musical journalism are also frequent sources of contributive income to composers. They seldom provide a full living. The only kind of written musical criticism that really feeds its writer is a permanent post on a metropolitan daily. Musical composition seems to be quite impossible to combine with such a full-time job. In any case, these "major" critics never seem to write any music, not the way dramatic critics write plays. Writing occasional articles, however, is an inveterate habit of composers. The profession is incurably literate. Such writing is interesting to the musical public, because it is both authoritative and passionately prejudiced. It is interesting to the composer because he can use it to logroll for his friends and to pay off old scores against his enemies, as well as to clarify for himself periodically his own aesthetic prejudices. Also, the forced attendance at concerts that writing criticism entails keeps him informed of current trends in musical production. Left to himself, he has rather a tendency to avoid hearing music, to insulate himself against all currents and to fecundate in a vacuum. Now a vacuum is not a very good place to fecundate in; at least it is not a good place to cook up collaborative art. Daily intercourse with other men's music deforms any composer's work in the direction of a rather timid traditionalism. Such is the music of the schoolteachers, the choir-masters, the touring virtuosos, and the conductors. But a complete ignorance of what is going on in the world of music is even more deforming. One doesn't so much need to know what the other composers are up to as one needs to know what the interpreters are up to. One needs to keep in touch with what happens when scores get made audible.

Painters can fecundate in a vacuum, if they really have to; the naïve painters are numerous and often not bad. Poetry too can flourish far from the madding crowd and often does, going off periodically into hermit-like retirement being quite a habit of poets. Think too of all the excellent lyrical verse that gets written year after year by private persons. Music, even naïve music, has always been written in or near the great centers of musical activity. The isolated composer, like the isolated surgeon or architect, is a rare animal.

As I said before, contributive sources of income seldom

influence a composer's stylistic orientation. Only a full support can do that. Their chief influence is technical. Just as a little teaching is good for any musical executant, and a little musical execution for any composer, a little criticism is a valuable experience too for any musician. It teaches him about audiences. Nobody who has ever tried to explain in writing why some piece got a cold reception that he thought merited better, or why some musical marshmallow wowed them all has ever failed to rise from his desk a wiser man. And the composer who has written musical criticism with some regularity, who has faced frequently the deplorable reality that a desired audience-effect cannot be produced by wishful thinking, inevitably, unconsciously, in spite of his most disdainful intentions, cannot help learning a good deal that is practical to know about clarity, coherence, and emphasis.

Composers' criticism is useful to the layman also. As I have said before, the function of criticism is to aid the public in digesting musical works. Not for nothing does it so often resemble bile. The first process in that digestion is the breaking-up of any musical performance into its constituent elements, design and execution. In this analytic process, the composer is of the highest utility. All musicians can judge the skill of a musical execution, because all musicians are executants. (The practice of publishing musical criticism written by musical illiterates is disappearing from even the provincial press.) But if the critic is only an executant and has never practiced musical creation, his interest is held far more by the refinements of execution than by the nature of the music itself. Inevitably he tends to glorify the executant (with whom he identifies himself imaginatively) and to neglect or to take for granted the piece played. Because of the fact that performers advertise and composers don't, the criticism of composition in the musical trade-weeklies is a complimentary gesture only and is extremely limited in space. Even the daily press, for all its official good will toward novelty, cannot get around the fact that the work of prosperous persons like conductors, opera-singers, and touring virtuosos has more "news-value" than the work of composers, most of whom don't even make a living from their work. So that inevitably most musical criticism is written from the performer's point of view.

The composer-critic identifies himself imaginatively with the author of any work he hears. He knows exactly (or has a pretty good idea) when the composer and the interpreter are in the groove and when they are getting in each other's hair. He is likely to be a shade indifferent about execution, unless the latter is quite out of keeping with the style of the work executed. Nevertheless, he does know about execution, in addition to knowing about design; and he can explain to others wherein their pleasure or displeasure is due to the design and wherein the execution and where to a marriage of the two.

The criticism of poetry is written nowadays almost exclusively by poets for other poets to read. It is highly technical and bitterly controversial. The layman scarcely ever sees it. It has nothing to do with any absorptive process among the reading public, because there isn't any reading public for poetry. The criticism of painting is written by collectors, museum-directors, and dealers' hired men. Since a painting is a piece of property and hence always belongs to somebody, any criticism written by the person it belongs to or by anybody connected with him or by anybody who has a rival picture or kind of picture to sell or who makes his living by showing pictures or by advising buyers, is about as interesting as musical criticism would be if it were written by the director of the Columbia Concerts Corporation or by an employee of the NBC Artists Service. When painters write about one another they are nasty; they lack even that commercial courtesy that dealers' representatives preserve toward one another. Prefaces to the catalogues of dealers' shows are usually blurbs by unemployed poets; they are not even paid advertising. The writing of art-history (which is criticism too, of course) is more reliable. At least it is when it is written by scholars with a steady job and no dealer- or museum-connections. On the whole, there just is no criticism of contemporary painting and not very much of poetry. There is only blurb and bitterness.

Music, theater, and architecture have a copious literature of contemporary criticism, because they have, to begin with, a public, and because that public is essentially disinterested. It doesn't own works of music or plays; and works of architecture, though they are real property, are not often owned by the persons who use them. The dominating rôle in this copious literature of criticism is played by the composers, the dramatic authors, and the architects themselves. Dancing and the movies have also a good public, and lots of criticism of them gets published. Most of it, unfortunately, is either trivial or venal, because choreographers and cinema-directors, the only people who know anything about design in their respective arts, have so far mostly kept out of it. (An exception is Pare Lorentz, America's number-one movie-critic, who has become a successful and distinguished director of non-fictional films.)

No art in its first expansive period needs criticism anyway. There isn't time to bother with anything but creation and distribution. With further expansion of the movie-trades momentarily arrested by international trade-wars, by financial crises, and by the menace of television, a certain amount of soul-searching does go on in the movie-world; and a few historical books have been written. It is quite certain that if the movies continue to function as an entertainment-form we shall see an increasing amount of critical writing about them from persons experienced in their making.

[g.] *The Appreciation-racket*

Every composer is approached from time to time by representatives of the Appreciation-racket and offered money to lecture or to write books about the so-called Appreciation of Music. Unless he is already tied up with the pedagogical world, he usually refuses. If he makes his living as a teacher, refusal is difficult. I've seen many a private teacher forced out of business for refusing to "co-operate" with the publishers of Appreciation-books. Refusal of public-school credits for private music-study is the usual method of foreclosure. The composer who teaches in any educational institution except a straight conservatory is usually obliged to "co-operate." The racket muscles in on him. His name will be useful; his professional prestige will give a coloration of respectability to the shady business. He is offered a raise and some security in his job. He usually accepts.

Every branch of knowledge furnishes periodically to the layman digests of useful information about that branch of knowledge and elementary hand-books of its technique. Simplified explanations of the copyright laws, of general medicine for use in the home, of the mathematics of relativity, of how to build a canoe, a radio-set, or a glider, of home dressmaking, of garden-lore, of how to acquaint yourself with classical archaeology in ten volumes, and of how to see Paris in ten days—this literature is in every way legitimate. Some of the most advanced practitioners in every branch of knowledge have at one time or another paused to write down in non-technical language what was going on in those branches. The artistic professions have a large literature of this sort, the present book being an example. Biographies of celebrated musicians, histories of the symphony orchestra with descriptions of the commoner instruments, synopses of opera plots, memoirs of singers and their managers, even of musical hostesses, all go to swell the general knowledge about music and how it lives. Works of a scholarly or pedagogical nature, like treatises on harmony, on acoustics, on instrumentation, or bibliographies of historical documents, need no justification at all. They are instruments for the direct transmission of professional knowledge.

What needs some explaining is the Appreciation-literature, which transmits no firm knowledge and describes no real practice. The thing nearest like it is the physical culture advertisement that proposes to augment the muscularity and the virile forces of any customer who will buy the book and do what it says for five minutes a day. Obviously, five minutes a day of gymnastics, any kind of gymnastics, with or without a book, will inside a week produce a temporary enlargement of the muscles exercised. Equally, the deliberate listening to music, any kind of music, five minutes a day for a week will sharpen momentarily the musical listening-ability. If the Appreciation-racket were no more than a pretext for habituating listeners to musical sounds, it would be a legitimate advertising device, destined, with luck, to swell the number of possible concert-customers.

What distinguishes it from the physical culture schemes is the large number of reputable musicians, philanthropic foundations, and institutions of learning connected with it and the large amounts of finance-capital behind it. So much money and so much respectability behind a business that hasn't very much intrinsically to recommend it is, to say the least, suspect.

When I say the books of Music-Appreciation transmit no firm knowledge and describe no real practice, you will either believe me or you won't. I have no intention of exposing in detail here the operating methods of that sinister conspiracy or of attacking by name the distinguished musicians who have signed its instruments of propaganda. If you are a musician, all I need say is, just take a look at the books. If you are not, avoid them as you would the appearance of evil.

It is as difficult for the layman to avoid contact with Music-Appreciation as it is for the musician. Children in elementary schools get it handed out to them along with their sight-singing. So far as it is just a substitution of European folklore for American folklore and made-up exercises, not much real harm is done. At least, not as long as the center of attention remains instruction in sight-singing rather than the tastefulness of the pieces sung. It is in the secondary schools, with the introduction into education of mere listening, that is to say, of a passive musical experience, to replace performance, which is an active experience, that Appreciation begins to rear its ugly head. In secondary schools, especially in those where instruction is accomplished according to the pedagogic devices known as Progressive Education, passivity seems to be the chief result sought. A proper, that is to say, an enthusiastic, receptivity to canned musical performance is highly prized by "progressive" educators.

In colleges the Appreciation of Music is a snap course, and as such it fills a need for many a busy (or lazy) student. As anything else it is hard to defend. For professional music-students it is confusing, because the explanations are esthetic rather than technical; and esthetics are a dangerous waste of time for young practical musicians. What they need is musical analysis and lots of execution according to the best living traditions of execution. For non-professional students also it is a waste of time that might be spent on musical practice. The layman's courses for adults in ordinary civil life are an abbreviated version of the collegiate Appreciation-courses. They offer nothing more (technically) than could be learned in one music lesson from any good private teacher. The rest is a lot of useless and highly inaccurate talk about fugues and sonata-form, sales-talk for canned music really.

The basic sales-trick in all these manifestations is the use of the religious technique. Music is neither taught nor defined. It is preached. A certain limited repertory of pieces, ninety per cent of them a hundred years old, is assumed to contain most that the world has to offer of musical beauty and authority. I shall explain in a moment how this repertory is chosen by persons unknown, some of them having no musical authority whatsoever. It is further assumed (on Platonic authority) that continued auditive subjection to this repertory harmonizes the mind and sweetens the character, and that the conscious paying of attention during the auditive process intensifies the favorable reaction. Every one of these assumptions is false, or at least highly disputable, including the Platonic one. The religious technique consists in a refusal to allow any questioning of any of them. Every psychological device is used to make the customer feel that musical non-consumption is sinful. As penance for his sins he must:

A. Buy a book.
B. Buy a gramophone.
C. Buy records for it.
D. Buy a radio.
E. Subscribe to the local orchestra, if there is one.

As you can see, not one of these actions is a musical action. They are at best therapeutic actions destined to correct the customer's musical defects without putting him through the labors of musical exercise. As you can see also, they entail spending a good deal more money than a moderate amount of musical exercise would entail. Persons whose viscera are not audito-sensitive need very little musical exercise anyway. To make them feel inferior for not needing it and then to supply them with musical massage as a substitute for what they don't need is, although a common enough commercial practice, professionally unethical.

If you will look at almost any of the Appreciation-books you will notice:

A. That the music discussed is nearly all symphonic. Chamber-music (except string-quartets) and the opera are equally neglected.

B. That the examples quoted are virtually the same in all the books.

C. That they are quoted from a small number of musical authors.

D. That 90% of them were written between 1775 and 1875 and are called Symphony Number Something-or-Other.

All this means that by tacit agreement Music is defined as the instrumental music of the Romantic era, predominantly symphonic and predominantly introspective. At least that that repertory contains a larger amount of the "best" music than any other. This last assumption would be hard to defend on any grounds other than the popularity of the symphony orchestras (plus their gramophone recordings and radio transmissions) performing this repertory.

A strange thing this symphonic repertory. From Tokio to Lisbon, from Jerusalem to Seattle, ninety per cent of it is the same fifty pieces. The other ten is usually devoted to good-will performances of works by local celebrities. All the rest is standardized. So are the conductors, the players, the soloists. All the units of the system are interchangeable. The number of first-class symphony orchestras in the world is well over a thousand. Europe, exclusive of the Soviet Union, counts more than two hundred. Japan alone is supposed to have forty. They all receive state, municipal, or private subvention; and the top fifty all have gramophone- and radio-contracts. All musical posts connected with them are highly honorific. Salaries, especially for conductors and management, are the largest paid anywhere today in music. The symphony orchestras are the king-pin of the international music-industry. Their limited repertory is a part of their standardization. The Appreciation-racket is a cog in their publicity machine.

It is not my intention here to go into the virtues and defects of the system beyond pointing out that the standardization of repertory, however advantageous commercially, is not a result of mere supply and demand. It has been reached by collusion between conductors and managers and is maintained mostly by the managers, as everybody knows who has ever had anything to do with the inside of orchestral concerts. To take that practical little schematization of Romanticism for the "best" in music is as naïve as taking chain-store groceries for what a gourmet's merchant should provide. For a composer to lend the prestige of his name and knowledge to any business so unethical as that is to accept the decisions of his professional inferiors on a matter gravely regarding his profession. I do not know whether it would be possible to publish a book or offer a course of instruction in music-appreciation that would question the main assumptions of the present highly organized racket and attempt to build up a listener's esthetic on other assumptions. I doubt if it would, and the experience of various well-intentioned persons in this regard tends to support my doubts. Their attempts to disseminate musical knowledge among musically illiterate adults seem to have led them eventually to substitute for instruction in listening some exercise in musical execution, such as choral singing or the practice of some simple instrument like the recorder. It would seem that such execution, which, however elementary, is a positive musical act, gives not only its own pleasure of personal achievement but also no inconsiderable insight into the substance of all music.

Do not confuse the Appreciation-racket with the practice of musical analysis or with the exposition of musical history. These are legitimate matters for both students and teacher to be occupied with. I am talking about a real racket that any American can recognize when I describe it. It is a fake-ecstatic, holier-than-thou thing. Every school and college, even the most aristocratically anti-musical, is flooded with it. Book-counters overflow with it. Mealy-mouthed men on the air serve it in little chunks between the numbers of every symphony-orchestra concert broadcast. It is dispensed in high academic places by embittered ex-composers who don't believe a word of it. It is uncritical, in its acceptance of imposed repertory as a criterion of musical excellence. It is formalist, in its insistence on preaching principles of sonata-form that every musician knows to be either non-existent or extremely inaccurate. It is obscurantist, because it pretends that a small section of music is either all of music or at least the heart of it, which is not true. It is dogmatic, because it pontificates about musical "taste." Whose taste? All I see is a repertory chosen for standardization purposes by conductors (who are musicians of the second category) and managers (who are not even musicians), and expounded by unsuccessful pianists, disappointed composers, and all the well-meaning but irresponsible little school-teachers who never had enough musical ability to learn to play any instrument correctly.

The musical ignorance of the army of teachers that is employed to disseminate Appreciation should be enough to warn any musician off it. Most composers are wary at first. Then it becomes tempting, because the money looks easy; and they think they at least will not be disseminating ignorance. Also in academic posts there is considerable straight pressure brought to bear. Nine times out of ten the young composer who is trying to make a modest living out of teaching harmony or piano-playing is ordered to get up a course in Appreciation (the tonier institutions are now calling it Listening) whether he wants to or not. He can make his own decision, of course; but I am telling him right now what will happen if he gets caught in those toils. He will cease to compose.

It always happens that way. No professional man can give himself to an activity so uncritical, so obscurantist, so dogmatic, so essentially venal, unless he does it to conceal his fundamental sterility, or unless he does it with his tongue in his cheek. In the latter case he gets out of it pretty quick. In the former case he gets out of composition instead. He gets out with some regret, because his professional status is lowered. But there is nothing to be done about that. Appreciation-teaching is not even a Special Skill of any kind. It is on the level of Minimum Musicality, as everybody in music knows.

So your composer who sticks at it becomes an ex-composer and an embittered man. Always beware of ex-composers. Their one aim in life is to discourage the writing of music.

¶4. *The Just Rewards of His Labor.*

This brings me to the last kind of composers' income, namely, receipts from his own musical works as published, performed, or recorded. It is sad that these should come last. If they were not so rare they would naturally have come first. Well, the facts are the facts. Performing-rights fees and royalties on copies sold are about the last thing any composer need ever expect to live on. His children sometimes come in for a bit of gravy. (The heirs of Ethelbert Nevin are doing quite well, thank you.)

I had better explain here something about royalties and performing-rights fees. Printed music brings to its composer (theoretically) a fee of ten per cent of the marked retail price for every copy sold. I say theoretically, because many publishers don't pay anything to the author. They think they are doing enough for him when they publish his work at all. If he pays the expenses of publication, he is usually allowed his ten per cent royalty. Gramophone recordings also bring to the composer a royalty of so much per record sold. This fee is generally paid. The performing-rights fees of published music are currently shared between the publisher and the composer. If a piece has words, the author of the words comes in for a part of the composer's share.

There exist in all Western countries mutual protective societies of composers, authors, and publishers, whose purpose in life is to enforce the payment of minimum performing-rights fees by producing organizations. In Europe these societies cover all the public usages of music, whether there is an admission-charge or not, by cinemas, theaters, broadcasting stations, opera houses, concert halls, churches, cafés, night-clubs, and municipalities. Even whore-houses and musical mendicants are not exempt from payment. In the United States the American Society of Composers, Authors, and Publishers, commonly known as ASCAP, functions similarly, but really covers not much except the usages of dance music and popular songs. Theatrical music is covered, by courtesy, through the Dramatists' Guild of the Authors' League of America. No performing-rights fees are collected in America at all, except by individual contract (which means there is no minimum payment), from symphony orchestras, traveling concert-artists, the major opera houses, the churches, schools, colleges, and clubs. In most cases of unpublished works in large form played by chamber or symphonic organizations, no fee is paid to the composer at all, not even a rental fee for the use of score and parts. This situation will not long continue, but for the present it is the case. It is the unique and sole reason for the existence in Europe of a much larger number of art-composers who live off their just share in the profits of the commercial exploitation of their work than exists in the United States. Such composers are almost non-existent in America. Let us call them, for the sake of brevity, successful composers (successful being understood here to mean earning a living by writing music).

Of all the composing musicians, this group presents in its music the greatest variety both of subject-matter and of stylistic orientation, the only limit to such variety being what the various musical publics at any given moment will take. Even the individual members of the group show variety in their work from piece to piece. This variety is due in part to their voluntary effort to keep their public interested and to enlarge their market. (Stylistic "evolution" is good publicity nowadays.) A good part of it is due also to the variety of usages that are coverable by commercially ordered music. Theater, concert, opera, church, and war demand a variety of solutions for individual esthetic cases according to the time, the place, the subject, the number and skill of the available executants, the social class, degree of musical cultivation, and size of the putative public. Music made for no particular circumstance or public is invariably egocentric. Music made for immediate usage, especially if that usage is proposed to the composer by somebody who has an interest in the usage, is more objective and more varied.

Successful composers are often accused of repeating themselves. In real truth they repeat themselves less often than the unsuccessful ones do. The latter keep writing the same piece over and over in the hope they can make it clearer next time, make people understand somehow. Successful men are often accused of "compromising," too, of compromising with public taste (which is assumed to be bad taste and profitable to cater to). I assure you that first-string composers have reputations to keep up, and that anyone who has a paying public (however small) is less tempted to "write down" to that public than the prize-and-commission winners are to "write up" to musical snobs. I also assure you that public taste is not necessarily bad taste, any more than private taste is necessarily good taste, and that the quickest way for a successful composer to stop being a success is for him to vulgarize his work. Success is like travel; it broadens a man, makes him at once more objective and more passionate about the things that matter to him. There must be inconveniences about living off the just rewards of one's labor, but I don't know what they are. I have never known an artist of any kind who didn't do better work when he got properly paid for it.

The composer who lives on music-writing invariably tends toward the theater. Handel and Verdi and Gershwin are classic examples. I do not know, in the past two or three hundred years, of any composer who has lived for very long off the commercial profits of symphonic and chamber music. The song-writers don't do too badly, and certainly Richard Strauss receives, now that he is old, a respectable income from his non-operatic music. But by and large, the theater is where the money is and where most of the composers are who have once had a taste of that money. Movies, opera, incidental music, ballet, these are the musical forms that feed their man. Composers who get fed by them have plenty of time to write a more disinterested music if they wish. Many do. All I am saying is that the commercially successful professional composer (and by commercially successful I mean he eats) is likely to be a theater man. That is his occupational deformity, if any.

¶ *To sum up and conclude:*

Every composer's music reflects in its subject-matter and in its style the source of the money the composer is living on while writing that music. This applies to introspective music as well as to objective.

The quality of any piece of music is not a function of its author's income-source. One has only to remember history to know otherwise. J. S. Bach and César Franck were church organists. Handel and Verdi and Gluck and Rameau were theater men. Beethoven skimped along on patronage and publishers' fees. Wagner (after his exile) and Tchaikovsky lived on gifts. Chopin and Liszt were concert-pianists and gave lessons. Mendelssohn and Brahms were gentlemen of means. Haydn received a salary for writing music and for organizing musical entertainments at the country house of one Count Esterházy. Schumann was a musical journalist. A great many modern composers are pedagogues. One might mention Hindemith, Schoenberg, d'Indy, and practically all the Americans. Krenek and Chavez are conductors. Satie was a post-office employee, Moussorgsky a customs official, Cui a chemist. Mozart did everything in music at one time or another except journalism. Palestrina and Debussy lived on their musical receipts till they got tired of starving and married rich widows. One could go on, but I think this should be enough to show that excellent music can be written on almost any kind of money.

Anyone who wishes to follow this matter through musical history in more detail is warned not to consider contributive income as very important. It amplifies a composer's practical experience, when it has to do with music; but it does not determine either his style or his subject-matter. Nothing does that but what he is actually living on. Nothing impresses a man very deeply except what pays him a living wage.

CHAPTER EIGHT

COMPOSERS' POLITICS, or

Professional bodies versus the secular state

LET us do a little more summing-up before we go on.

The composer is a neat little man who lives in a hotel-room and has charming manners. His neatness, like that of the engineers, is due to the fact that exactitude, in his profession, pays receipts. His charming manners are a result of his multiple civil status. As an executant musician or as a teacher, he is a laboring man, a time-worker, a union-member, a white-collar proletarian, skilled in class warfare and trained to conceal his class feelings. As a composer he belongs to the bourgeois Professional Classes, with all that that means of pride and intellectual authority. As the author of published or frequently played works, he is a small proprietor who leases out his property-rights for exploitation by commercial interests. In these last two capacities, he enjoys the greatest access to culture and the greatest freedom of thought that our century has to offer, that of the petty bourgeoisie. As son or husband, he is not infrequently a private capitalist, a man of means, with all the freedom of action that only an unearned income can give. Is it any wonder that his ways are gracious and that his tongue is smooth? Is it any wonder that the manner of his work should change from year to year and even from month to month as the play of these class forces gives first one and then another the dominant financial rôle in his life.

The nature of these variations we have just described. How a non-musical job produces non-traditional music. How an inherited income that is big enough to live on produces music that reflects the censorships and preoccupations of the investing classes, music that is delicate, frivolous, introspective, or vulgar, as delicacy, frivolity, introspection, or vulgarity are being done at any given time in those circles. How a married income is likely to interrupt the function of composition altogether, or else to act on the composer in the same way as any other direct subvention or patronage. These last would seem to produce revolt-music, excepting in the case of special awards and commissions, which, to the contrary, produce a quite rigid sort of international conformism. Pedagogy makes for complication, musical execution for brilliance, criticism for the wow-technique. Traffic with the Appreciation-racket produces sterility. Living on the rewards of one's labors as a composer would seem to be the preferable situation, even though that entails almost inevitably doing a certain amount of theatrical work, held by many musicians (incorrectly, I think) to be slightly lowering. Unfortunately and very curiously, considering the enormous quantities of art-music consumed every year all over the world, the composer who lives by composing is a rare animal.

Let me remind you once more that when I speak of a source of income I mean a source that produces enough income to live on. Let me remind you also that with the exception of being able to live on the receipts from the exploitation of one's music, which seems really to improve the quality of a composer's work, and of trafficking with the Appreciation-racket, which is death, no money is any better or any worse than any other money. The source of the money, however, what the composer has to do to get it or to keep it, produces a certain occupational deformity, a stylistic conditioning. That is all. Perfectly good music, music of the highest excellence, always has been written, and still is, under any of these conditionings.

So far we have considered the composer's individual

behavior. Let us now look at his group movements. What are his politics, for instance; and what does he do about them?

Let me make clear right at the start what I mean by political words. I shall try to use them all in the way they are most commonly understood, I think, by English-speaking people, avoiding, where possible, usages that are still confined to sectarian groups. A political policy is a program of government, an impersonal thing. Politics is the wangle about who executes it, a personal thing. To put it more briefly, policy is what you do and politics is who does it. Political principles are impersonal. They are ideas, something people think and talk about. Political action is personal. It is what any man really does to change economic or social conditions. It is not necessarily in accord with what he thinks are his political principles. In order that political action be effective on the part of private citizens, it must of necessity be group action. Group action always entails joining something. Time-workers and piece-workers join trade-unions. Craft-workers in the arts call their unions guilds or alliances. Small proprietors and professional men call theirs associations. Capitalists call theirs Institutes or Leagues.

Policy, which is a line of conduct, what is actually being done, or is capable of being done, in any given society or class of same, is a mysterious quantity. Sometimes it is discussed in advance, sometimes not. Sometimes it is the result of reflection on the part of a small group of persons. Sometimes it is the expression of unanimous public desire and is not reflected about at all, because the thing to be done seems to everybody an obvious and proper thing to do. But whether a certain line of policy is taken spontaneously or is imposed by a small and self-conscious group, it has no necessary relation whatever to the persons governing or holding office during the time that policy is in effect. This dichotomy is particularly noticeable in societies which have a visible parliamentary procedure and some popular voting. In nineteenth-century England, for example, the formula of social reform was that the Liberals proposed changes and agitated for them, but that the opponents of such changes, the Conservatives, actually voted most of them into law and administered the new mechanisms.

I realize that I am venturing here quite unprotected on the disputed ground of how history gets made. I realize also that I am not giving much consideration to the purely personal weight of certain men in power at certain times. It seems to me that the cases of a Julius Cæsar, a Charlemagne, a Louis XIV, a Napoleon, a Lenin, a Hitler, are more spectacular than frequent. Crystallizations of events take place around them, perhaps even within them. The sluggish stream of history rolls on for the most part quite independent of who is riding any visible raft at any given moment.

Politics is the business of raft-riding. In the so-called democratic countries it is operated on a two-party system. These two parties, variously named in different countries and frequently subdivided, are always only two, the ins and the outs. There is complete collusion between them, as we all know. The only serious points of difference have to do with patronage (who gets what job) and responsibility (who gets the buck passed to him when a particularly unpleasant bit of work is about to be done). The procedure is the same under the so-called autocratic governments, only the ins and the outs don't call themselves two parties. In modern autocracies, any form of organization among the outs is discouraged; and the word party is used only by the ins.

All this explanation may seem a bit unnecessary and obvious. Certainly it is not original with me. It is, I think, the philosophy of history and government most commonly accepted today among persons who have any philosophy of history and government at all.

The workings of practical politics, that is to say, of office-holding, touch the composer's life very little today in England and the United States, because there are virtually no jobs open there to musicians on state or federal pay-rolls. The W.P.A. offers some; and the procedure for getting them is not unlike that for getting government art-jobs in Mexico and on the European Continent, where the state subvention of music and music-education brings an enormous number of posts connected with these into the pattern of bureaucratic administration. It might be interesting to examine the effect of government job-holding on musical style. I do not have any very firm ideas on the subject. I have never been able to put my finger on a case where I could note any influence at all. There is a little, perhaps, on the choice of objective literary subject-matter. But the sources of style (and of introspective subject-matter too) are what you do to earn money, not who signs the pay-check. A harmony-teacher is a harmony-teacher and a conductor a conductor, whether he works for a government bureau or for a private foundation. He is only different when he works for a students' or an executants' co-operative. There is probably a trifle more of intellectual and esthetic freedom for everybody under a bureaucratic set-up than there is under the privately financed musical set-up of England and the United States. Certainly all tendencies toward dogmatic conservatism on the part of state-supported musicians seem to produce by reaction all sorts of vigorous corrective tendencies among those who do not have state jobs. The only difference between the democratic and the autocratic countries in this matter is that in the more authoritarian cultures, the corrective tendencies flourish under cover (or in exile). A great deal of the more advanced German music is now written in the United States, for instance; and we hear that in Vienna American swing music, which has the civil status of prohibition alcohol, is consumed passionately in musical speakeasies.

All this is preliminary to the question of what are the composer's politics. The composer's political action, like his musical style, is determined by his chief income-source. By political action I mean what he does in a group to conserve or to improve his economic privileges. State job-holding has to do with party politics; and although it is quite as legitimate as any other form of job-holding, it is not a form of political action. Joining a union of state job-holders is a political action. Neither is voting a political action. It is too private, for one thing. For another, it has nothing to do with governmental policy. It has only to do with the choice of political executants. As political action it is cart-before-horse.

We hear about musicians voting for this and that candidate or party ticket. A great many of them, I assure you, don't vote at all. We hear also a great variety of opinions expressed in the music world about foreign policy and about many other matters that citizens are not allowed to vote on. Of direct political action one sees a good deal too, but often it is in no way related to the musician's voting or to his political talking, which are just ornamental camouflage and vary mostly according to the neighborhood the musician lives in.

Let us take up the income-sources in order again:

The naïf, the non-professional composer, takes his political action with whatever group he gets his living from or among.

The composer who lives on inherited capital is solidly with the investors always. He may join the Musicians' Union for protective reasons. He is not a union-minded man. In any dispute between the union and the management he sides with the management.

The composer who lives on married money, like the composer who lives on personal subventions, is of a divided mind. A poor man himself, he is anti-rich. But as a tolerated member of the wealthy classes, though he is granted lots of pleasant perquisites, he is not allowed to do anything opposed to their interests. The resulting tension comes out in his music as the revolt-tendency I mentioned before. In his conversation he pretends a great sympathy for the underdog. In union matters he always sides with capital. But take his income away and his stored-up hatred of the rich, plus his intimate knowledge of their ways, makes him a leader in class warfare.

The subventioned composer acts politically just like the one who marries this income. They are both kept-men. The subvention must, however, be enough to keep him. One hundred dollars a month of well-assured income is about the minimum. If the subvention goes lower than that, or if it seems likely to terminate at any moment, his mentality is not that of the kept-man any more, but of the chronically unemployed; and his political action at such moments follows that of the unemployed masses. The Home Relief dole, for instance, is an insufficient subvention. Work Relief (the W.P.A.), which pays $93.86 a month, is just sufficient to count as a subvention; and it does so count for the easel-painters. The only reason why it doesn't for composers is that there is not yet any provision in the Federal Music Project for free musical composition. All the composers in the W.P.A. are doing a specified musical work of some kind. They are earning the salary they are living on and hence feel no need for personal revolt.

The conductors and the concert artists make a show of political conservatism. They are impressed by money and hanker for the sumptuous life. They express horror at the musical ignorance of the masses, imagine themselves as Haydn *bei* Esterházy or as Leonardo at the Court of Francis I. They think they own Musical Taste, should be allowed to administer this as a Vested Right, and be handsomely paid for doing so. They even vote with the rich. But underneath all this ornamental glub-glub they are solidly anti-capital. In union disputes they almost never take the producer's side. They either take the proletarian side or shut up, because they are completely dependent for their livelihood on the good will of union musicians. The American Guild of Musical Artists is hot on the warpath these days to cut down management commissions, to establish basic-minimum contracts with impresarios, and to collect royalties on the sale of gramophone records. The financial interests are opposing all this, naturally; but your high-class musical artist is out for blood. Like a petted darling who is no longer being petted, his fury knows no bounds toward the class that refuses to pet. He is a little disdainful still of the more proletarian musicians' union, but at every turn he is obliged to accept their help and to offer in return his solidarity. In private life he continues to frequent the rich and to express his distaste for the musical *polloi*.

The critics are conversationally either Marxian or Machiavellian. In action they are all very much alike. They have no craft union and no professional body. A few belong to the Newspaper Guild. Those of them who really earn their living by criticism are tied up, heart, voice, and hand, with the symphony-orchestra interests, which means the radio and gramophone interests, which means in turn the electrical-patents-and-banking combine.

The teachers are trade-unionists. School-teachers love joining unions, and they run their unions with a minimum of venality. The French school-teachers' union is the hard-headedest, the most independent, and the most determined group in the General Labor Confederation. The teachers' unions in America, although quite radical in their principles and often firm in action, are devoured by a desire to have everybody understand that their members are not just ordinary laboring men. They are doomed to disappointment. They are white-collar proletarians and nothing else. That a good deal of teaching, especially advanced teaching, should be done by master workmen is necessary and inevitable. That a teacher has any knowledge or training which raises him above the position that is his on account of what he actually knows about some subject, I deny. I mean that pedagogy is not a profession like musical composition, nor even a trade like piano-playing. It has no traditions, no body of esoteric knowledge, no special skill, and no authority. All any teacher knows over and above such real knowledge as he may have of his subject is a half-dozen rules of thumb that anybody can learn in fifteen minutes. I don't mean to say one teacher isn't a more skillful pedagogue than another. Quite the contrary. I mean no system of pedagogy is any better than any other. The fact that there are so many systems on the market (they are as numerous in America as religions) means that there is no tradition. If the teacher knows his subject and keeps his temper, the student can usually be depended on to get everything out of him that he can digest.

There is no way around it. The school-teachers, much as they would like to be considered an intellectual caste, are really white-collar proletarians; and politically they act as such. They vote with their intellectual neighborhood, as everybody else does, their particular neighborhood being principally left-liberal. Their organized activities are aimed at getting some kind of authority over school curricula and at defending their salaries and their tenure of office from the depredations of trustees and schoolboards, who represent in such disputes the profit motive and the authoritarian methods of finance-capital.

Getting mixed up with the Appreciation-racket, which is practically a political action in itself, is as suicidal to the composers' group as it is to the individual musical author.

The composer who lives by his composition shows little difference between his political opinions and his political actions. His small but real independence renders camouflage unnecessary. Like most small proprietors, he is a liberal. He defends himself through professional guild-associations against the depredations of finance-capital, which is always attacking his professional integrity or his income. He joins up with music publishers (also, at present, mostly small proprietors) to enforce the payment of performing-rights fees by producing organizations. He acts with his publisher against the time-workers whenever his profit is in jeopardy. He pays his secretary and his copyists as little as he can, which is to say that, like any other manufacturer, he pays his helpers exactly what it would cost him to replace them.

So far we have been talking about direct political action. Indirect political action, such as membership in general political parties, the self-supporting composer tends rather to avoid. It lowers his standing in the profession and tends to lower the prestige of the profession itself. Fighting openly as a group for economic amelioration does not lower the prestige of the profession. On the contrary, every material advantage so gained serves to raise it in public esteem.

The political actions that professional men engage in outside the professional body always create dissension within the body and thus tend to fail of their purpose. I maintain that the only legitimate purpose of any political action is a group purpose, and that the members of all the professions belong more inalienably to their profession than they do to any other social group. This is unquestionably true of those professional men who live by the practice of their profession. Ever since 1929 (it began rather earlier in Germany), there has been a good deal of ostentatious joining, by composers in England, France, and America, of Communist Parties adhering to the Third International. In the past few years a large part of the public activity of these parties has had to do with foreign policy, a matter that concerns the musical profession only indirectly. This open recourse of composers to indirect political action began to produce in the mid-1930's (by the immutable laws of reaction) a similar activity by other composers in the opposite direction. An approximately equal number of them got openly mixed up with social reactionaries, and all of a sudden the profession was split asunder on matters not directly concerning it. Instead of presenting a united front to their respective governments for the purpose of pressing their just demands, they went around taking "stands" on foreign policy, the unionization of heavy industry, and soil-conservation. This happened in all the Western countries except Italy and Russia. Germany put a rather melodramatic stop to it in 1933. In England, France, and the United States some of it still goes on, though less than it did formerly. The upshot of all such activities everywhere was the same. Not a single economic advantage was gained by the composer for his profession or by the profession for him in any country during the years (now over, alas) when any economic group could have practically anything it asked for out of any government.

Having missed the train when it was going, there is now a tendency to huddle together and say how sad is the lot of the composer. If I may be allowed to pronounce a little sermon on that text, I should like to point out, from the model of the medical profession, just how professional solidarity really works when it works.

The professions derive their power in society from their intellectual autonomy. They are self-perpetuating bodies. They reproduce their kind without aid or interference and present themselves to the state through their professional organizations. These organizations determine all matters regarding the technique of professional education and professional practice. Their internal functioning is democratic. The term "republic of letters" is the description of an analogous ideal.

The business of any professional body is to administer the corpus of that profession's knowledge. An intellectual republic demands of its members a minimum standard of professional skill, a high degree of collaborative effort, and the acceptance of collaborative responsibility. It demands, therefore, of any political authority under which it lives complete intellectual autonomy. In return, it grants to the political authority (grants grudgingly, however, and hands over only under pressure) the right to control the social usages of professional knowledge. On the question, for instance, of whether there is or is not to be health insurance, music instruction in the slums, state theater, or a tri-borough bridge, the professional bodies who will be involved in the execution of those projects can only recommend. The political authority decides yes or no. When the political authority says yes, the professionals execute the project; and they execute it in their own way. When the political authority says no, the project is not executed. The state's bailiwick is (if we must) subject-matter; the profession's is technique.

Professions deal with the political authority as one state deals with another, which is to say diplomatically, open warfare and passive resistance being, of course, diplomatic moves like any other. The defining of public health, safety, and expediency, at any given moment, is the privilege, the duty of the state. The defining of truth, beauty, falsehood, and correct syntax is at all times the duty of the intellectual republic. The political state may be organized after any known theory of political economy or any imaginable symbolism. The intellectual state is always organized as a classless society that owns all its means of production and reproduction and administers these by the procedures commonly known as internal democracy, which means open discussion of everything and the voting on policies as well as persons.

By the firm practice of such intellectual autonomy, any profession can obtain from any political state public honor and economic privilege. By neglecting to run its own house and messing around with things that are unquestionably Cæsar's, it never fails to end in a state of economic *and intellectual* slavery.

The medical men and the engineers have done well by themselves on such a program. Even the German government handles them with gloves. The lawyers everywhere, having tampered too much with party politics, have lost practically all their intellectual prestige. They still make money; and they still have their dominant rôle in legislation in a few countries, though this cannot last very much longer if they continue to derive their chief income from political perquisites and from aiding the maneuvers of industrial banking. The poets enjoy no economic consideration in any Western society, because they have failed to make clear to the literary profession itself just what rôle they can play in literary life that other writers can't. They are pretty vague, as a matter of fact, about their rôle in both life and letters. Their intellectual integrity is still intact, however. They do nobody's intellectual dirty-work, as the journalists and the screen-writers do. The painters, the least organized of the artists, are economically subject to picture merchants and to the pseudo-philanthropic museum racket. (The museums seem to be responsible economically to everybody but the painters they expose.)

The music world has more solidarity than any of the other art worlds. A further organization is necessary at this time, however, if composers, the only possible governing group in any complete and authoritative organization of music, are to assume that responsibility. The executant musicians are allied with the American Federation of Labor, as is proper. Similar affiliations exist among European musicians. The composers have an elementary business-combine with publishers, which is all right too, but far from completely effective, even in Europe. If they do not demand and secure for themselves complete authority over professional ethics, professional education, and the standards of musical execution, they will shortly find themselves in the position of having these responsibilities assumed for them, formally and legally, by persons not competent to execute them properly, even by persons with non-musical axes to grind.

Already an enormous part of the world's musical activity is administered by a combine of conductors and businessmen. I refer to the international symphony-orchestra industry. Radio is even less professional in its standards. The cinema is in the hands of bankers, ex-journalists, and acting-directors; composers have no voice in the esthetic counsels of that enormous music-producing machine. Musical education is being quietly overpowered by the Appreciation-racket, a money-making scheme of less than doubtful musical value. (Can you imagine a reputable university offering a course in the Appreciation of Surgery, for example, or in How to Listen to Murder Trials?)

Correction of these very grave faults in our civilization must be organized by composers, and such organization must be led by the composers who make their living from composing. Only they have sufficient influence over their colleagues, and the energy necessary to carry the thing through. The others are timid and fatalistic, not daring to move a muscle, lest what they have be taken away. The school-teachers, with their habits of union-organization and their invaluable good manners in discussion, will be able seconds. The kept-boys will applaud from a distance. The journalists and lecturers will try to turn it into a publicity scheme. But only the musical-composition-supported can start it, run it, and carry it anywhere. They are very few in number.

This is the end of my sermon. This is the end of my disquisition on the composer as a political animal.

CHAPTER NINE

INTELLECTUAL FREEDOM, or

What can and cannot be censored

WE HAVE seen that both the subject-matter and the stylistic orientation of music are economically determined. That is to say, more specifically, that the melodic and rhythmic material, the contrapuntal manner, and the style of its instrumentation are nourishment symbols. Of all the musical elements, only form and, in part, harmony are subject to free choice on the part of the composer.

Harmony itself is partly a stylistic device; and, in so far as it is, it follows the same orientation as the melodic material, its polyphonic and instrumental clothing. That is to say, that the ornamental and expressive aspects of harmony, the throwing-in of chromatics and false notes, the degree to which charm, cuteness, and voluntary distortion are employed, are personal characteristics of the composer and are determined by the sources of his personal income. The more fundamental aspect of harmony, its architectural function in music, is less subject to personal variation, because the tonal substructure of musical form is as impersonal a thing as musical form itself.

Let me take an analogy from engineering. The decision to build a bridge at a certain place is dependent on the putative usage a bridge at that place would receive. Also on somebody's ability to pay for the building operations. Everything in the design that has to do with the bridge's putative usage, its structure for function and durability, is determined by the engineer's impersonal, objective knowledge of hydraulics, mathematical mechanics, and the specific strengths of materials. This basic design would be not much different no matter who were paying for the bridge. The decorative covering, however, or the lack of it, the materials and design of the visible surfacing, are symbolic representations of the source of the bridge's financing. Private and municipal constructions have more decorative variety than those financed by railways or by corporate bond-issues. The latter make a great show of their strength lines, of their avoidance of the old-fashioned picturesque. Such surfacing is comparable to the visible material and style of a musical piece. The basic design of the bridge corresponds to what has always been called musical form. Musical form is functional planning, nothing else.

Harmony plays a cardinal rôle in such planning, the whole layout of the tonal syntax being the chief means by which coherence, clarity, and emphasis are achieved in a long piece. This layout is not personal or financial or emotional or charming or grandiose or cute. It is as professional as corset-making or skin-grafting. Real knowledge and a skilled hand are the determinants of success.

In the case of objective music, the content (the subject-matter) is chosen by the person who pays for that music to be written; and it is chosen for its appropriateness to the music's projected usage. Content's little brother, stylistic orientation, is made up (quite unconsciously) by the person who writes the music, as a symbolic representation of his personal attitude toward the income-source. It can even, if the client and the composer are in close accord, represent their mutual attitude toward an income-source. That stylistic orientation is expressed through the melodic material, its contrapuntal clothing, its harmonic and rhythmic ornamentation, and its instrumental coloring.

The form of music is chosen, or rather designed, by the composer to make the piece fulfill a specific function. This function is not invented by anybody usually; it is a social creation. Lest the word "form," which in the visual arts means rather the surface contours of a work than the structural devices for sustaining these, tend to signify stylistic matters in spite of our defining it otherwise, I prefer to speak of music's plan or design. That will avoid also a certain confusion that tends to arise from an unconscious comparison with poetry, whenever specific musical forms are referred to. Because music knows no such fixed forms as poetry does; there is nothing in music comparable to the sonnet, the triolet, the villanelle, the Spenserian stanza, the Alexandrine, *terza rima*. Even music with words rarely follows the metrical mold of its text with much exactitude. The strictest metrical conventions are those observed in music intended for use as accompaniment to social dancing. Music not intended for such usage, though it may call itself waltz, minuet, or pavane, makes no pretense to exact observance. About the only real conventions in music that could legitimately be called forms, and these are conventions of texture, not of meter, are the canon and the round. The much-taught fugue is far more a series of stylistic devices than it is a metrical or tonal formula, only the exposition section having any kind of stable convention about it.

The designing of music is always a practical matter. No composer pays any attention to the metrical conventions of poetic or dance forms unless by following them in songs or in dance pieces he can assure the utility of his music. For music of less specific intent, the possible usages are varied. They may take the form of a concert, of a whistled quotation, a religious ceremony, a sight-reading in the home, an adaptation to spectacular entertainment. Design in music is the planning of it for clarity of communication and for durability under the kind of usage specifically envisaged. Different specific usages of music require different subject-matters and certainly different styles; that is obvious. They also require different design-constructions. The cardinal determinant in music's structural design is length. The limits of this length, what is too short and what is too long, are determined by the social conventions that regulate the occasions of musical usage.

In the case of introspective music, neither the content nor the style is decided by anybody but the composer. These are entirely spontaneous, automatic, "inspired," though in the long run economically determined. They are not directly controllable by the composer or by anybody else. The designing of musical form, however, in all kinds of music, the planning for clarity, for function, and for durability, is not at all spontaneous or unconscious. Like all matters of grammar, syntax, and rhetoric, it is based on social convention and audience-psychology. All knowledge about it is empirical. Success comes from trial and error.

I should like to add here that the same empirical knowledge, the same objective calculation, enters into the procedure of instrumentation, but that that is not a calculation of audience-psychology. It is an adapting of the composer's personal thoughts to instrumental limitations and rule-of-thumb acoustics. In spite of the elaborate nature of its planning, instrumentation is primarily an emotional thing, a translation into sensuous terms of the visceral climate, the subconscious weather conditions in which the composer and his particular material feel most at home. That massive and colorful instrumentation is only incidentally an aid to clarity and emphasis is proved by the frequency with which these last seem to get preserved intact in piano-reductions of orchestral music.

And so to repeat. The composer in front of any subject-matter, whether that is objective or introspective, of any content and its stylistic implications, is passive, masochistic, egocentric. It grabs him by the scruff of the neck and makes him take dictation. The underpinning of all this with structural steel is the problem of musical design. Now a problem is objective, can only be solved by action, by sadistic experiment. The first process is like child-birth; practically anybody can do it. The second requires judgment, like the bringing-up of offspring. Decisions must be made continually.

I wanted to explain all this, which many people know

already (but which many don't), before examining the common musical usages. Because it is quite impossible to discuss aesthetics unless it is perfectly clear that there are in music-writing both voluntary and involuntary elements. The current schools of aesthetic criticism divide themselves, appropriately enough, along the lines of political philosophy. Let us call their spokesmen the scholastics, the big-business boys, and the Marxians. They all want to know how modern music gets that way. Also what, if anything, can be done about it.

The scholastics are the most informed about the history of stylistic detail. The conservative wing of them talks a great deal about "influences." They tell you who learned what from who, but say nothing about why Composer A, who knew everybody's music from B to Z, chose to imitate and to appropriate the formulas of C, H, and J rather than those of E, G, or W. They imply that personal idiosyncrasy determined the composer's ability or wish to accept such and such an influence. The more radical wing among the scholastics leans on *Kulturgeschichte*—finds music, painting, and architecture to be interrelated phenomena, all expressing, at any given period, the same *Zeitgeist*. Both wings are more convincing about the past than about the present, where personal stylistic variations always seem to surprise them.

The big-business boys, the Appreciation-school, are

completely hipped on sonata-form. They speak of it as if it were the key to musical knowledge and mastery of it the test of any composer's value. They even pretend that reading about this highly controversial subject will lead laymen to accept forcible feeding on symphonies. (The whole Appreciation-theory supposes an auditor in chains. It falls quite to pieces if he is physically and morally free, if he can be allowed, without committing an anti-social act, to leave the concert hall or radio-side and take up some diversion for which he has more liking.)

The Marxian school is hipped on the Revolutionary pattern. They have interesting views (though I think in many cases erroneous views) on how musicians should and do act politically. They tend to treat musical styles and usages as if they were a form of political action, which they are not. Musical style, like political action, is economically determined. The Marxians all know about that; at least, they ought to. Musical usages, however, are social customs. They transcend political and economic barriers. And the art of designing music to fit them must of necessity transcend these barriers too. Also, on questions of musical subject-matter the Marxians get nervous and moralistic.

Political theories have, in fact, very little more to do with musical creation than electronic theories have. Both merely determine methods of distribution. The exploitation of these methods is subject to political regulation, is quite rigidly regulated in many countries. The revolutionary parties, both in Russia and elsewhere, have tried to turn composers on to supposedly revolutionary subject-matter. The net result for either art or revolution has not been very important. Neither has official fascist music accomplished much either for music or for Italy or Germany.

Political party-influence on music is mostly just censorship anyway. Performances can be forbidden and composers disciplined for what they write, but the creative stimulus comes from elsewhere. Nothing really "inspires" an author but money or food or love.

That persons or parties subventioning musical uses should wish to retain veto power over the works used is not at all surprising. That our political masters (or our representatives) should exercise a certain negative authority, a censorship, over the exploitation of works whose content they consider dangerous to public welfare is also in no way novel or surprising. But that such political executives should think to turn the musical profession into a college of political theorists or a bunch of hired propagandists is naïve of them. Our musical civilization is older than any political party. We can deal on terms of intellectual equality with acoustical engineers, with architects, with poets, painters, and historians, even with the Roman clergy if necessary. We cannot be expected to take very seriously the inspirational dictates of persons or of groups who think they can pay us to get emotional about ideas. They can pay us to get emotional all right. Anybody can. Nothing is so emotion-producing as money. But emotions are factual; they are not generated by ideas. On the contrary, ideas are generated by emotions; and emotions, in turn, are visceral states produced directly by facts like money and food and sexual intercourse. To have any inspirational quality these must be present facts or immediate anticipations, not pie-in-the-sky.

Now pie-in-the-sky has its virtues as a political ideal, I presume. Certainly most men want to work for an eventual common good. I simply want to make it quite clear that ideals about the common good (not to speak of mere political necessity) are not very stimulating subject-matter for music. They don't produce visceral movements the way facts do. It is notorious that musical descriptions of hell, which is something we can all imagine, are more varied and vigorous than the placid banalities that even the best composers have used to describe heaven; and that all composers do better on really present matters than on either, matters like love and hatred and hunting and war and dancing around and around.

The moral of all this is that the vetoing of objective

subject-matter is as far as political stimulation or censorship can go in advance. Style is personal and emotional, not political at all. And form or design, which is impersonal, is not subject to any political differences of opinion.

The poets, who, like politicians, use words as their medium, are always disagreeing with politicians about political ideas. Composers don't so much. We are often asked to wonder how the composer, an intellectual, can accept life under an ignominious government. I assure you that that isn't the problem in censorious countries today. The problem is getting the government to accept you. If the composer can eat and work, accepting the government is easy as pie. All governments are ignoble, at least all I've ever seen or heard of.

Just as the painters are chiefly interested in depicting in two-dimensional paint how three-dimensional surfaces reflect light, the composers are chiefly interested in depicting by sound how their viscera face the facts of life. Hence they rarely get mixed up with government in their musical capacity. The Russian Association of Proletarian Musicians made a beautiful manifesto about musical style, made it three times, in fact. I recommend it to all to read. It was a witty and lifelike description of the immediate past. Its present musical program was of the vaguest, largely educational. Even at that, the Association was dissolved by government decree in 1932. Governments don't like professional states-within-the-state to play with cultural or with social policy.

There is a wave now in leftist circles of pretending that nothing in the world is outside the domain of politics. That is hooey. The ways of holding an audience's attention by musical sounds are not numerous. But they are in no way whatsoever connected with any political theory. The practice and transmission of such knowledge as exists about these is the business of the musical profession and must remain the business of the musical profession under any system of government. Advances in civilization (or even the maintenance of a status quo) depend not upon getting everything absorbed into politics, but on separating wherever possible and keeping separate from political tinkering all the knowledge there is about matters that are not any different no matter what political plans are on the fire.

Again I repeat. Subject-matter may interest politics, or it may not. If it does, the piece containing it may get censored. Works have been known to be censored too for their stylistic orientation, though very seldom. Usage may be ordered or forbidden by the powers that be or the powers that pay. Musical form, which is design for clarity, function, and durability, cannot possibly interest anybody but professionals.

CHAPTER TEN

HOW TO WRITE A PIECE, or

Functional design in music

I AM now going to list the commoner uses of music and describe some of the considerations that composers take account of when designing music for those uses.

THE DANCE-SONG

"Popular" music leaves the composer's hands in most cases as a song consisting of identical stanzas (known as "verses") and a refrain of thirty-two measures (known as the "chorus"). This is the basic "form" for publication and for professional transmission. Rarely does this "form" fail to be amplified in auditive usage. Frequently the verse disappears and the chorus becomes the whole tune. It is repeated with varying instrumentation for dancing, cut up and reharmonized for pianistic fun, distorted in stage-shows and movies to accompany acrobats, emotional scenes, and pageantry. The swing boys make fanciful variations on it for non-dancing listeners. A dozen completely different versions of the same title are sold as gramophone records or transmitted nightly by orchestras over the air.

The subject-matter in all these transformations is a thirty-two-measure tune. The musical style of its amplification and rendition is personal to every performer or performing group. The "form," usually a series of variations, is determined by each separate usage and fitted to whatever over-all timing is desired. The use of the variation series as a formula of composition comes from no high-brow motivation; it is simply that the variation series is the second simplest way of stretching any short piece of music out to fit a longer piece of time, the first and easiest way being exact repetition. Dance-players, church organists, and the leaders of military bugle corps don't hesitate to use exact repetition. It is not advisable, however, for jazz bands playing to seated auditors to repeat exactly, because both the band and the auditors would get bored.

The whole procedure of musical composition is evident in a lively way in the small improvisational swing groups. These employ a free contrapuntal style of playing, because it is easier to improvise counterpoint than harmony (unless you are playing a multiple-voiced instrument, like the piano or banjo or guitar, or an instrument with chord-buttons, like the accordion). The use of the variation series and wherever possible of the "imitative" style of counterpoint saves effort and gives coherence to the whole. The solo cadenza (called in swing jargon a "chorus") keeps up the interest of the players and produces the profitable rivalries that come from personal success. Each player takes a chorus to make it all seem fair and friendly, takes it when he feels like it, stops when through. All, so far, is unconscious, automatic. Where does reflection come in? What has to be decided on by somebody? Three things only. The tune, the time to start, and the time to stop. The first constitutes the subject of the music. The last two define the proportions of its form—the speed, intensity, and extent at which musical development within the variation series can take place. The variation series is not a form; it is a continuity device. The song-with-verse-and-chorus is a form, but one that exists chiefly on paper. In practice, the ten-inch disc, the three-minute swing number, the song-and-dance come as near being musical forms as so-called "popular" music has to offer, because they are at least bits of continuity within a dimension.

MUSIC AND PHOTOGRAPHY

As is well known, the movie was never a silent entertainment. The quiet tick-and-flicker of an unaccompanied film is dangerously soporific, no matter how clear the images or how exciting the narrative continuity. From the earliest days of the movies, the film-exhibitor has called in the aid of musical accompaniment to help him keep the house awake and to lend emotional poignancy to the dangerously frigid spectacle of a series of photographs. To this day the movies are dependent on music to hold the observer's attention and to direct his emotional responses. All of which means that the movie is a true musical form, as truly a musical form as the opera, though without as yet the opera's inseparable marriage of music to words.

Most descriptions of the movies are descriptions of the working methods by which they are made. I do not think these are immutable. Just because it is common practice to take the photographs and then to mount (or "cut") the film and finally to pin on some music, it does not follow that a film made after a musical composition could not be equally effective. The collaboration problem between movie-director and composer is not dissimilar, in fact, to that of the choreographer and the composer who make a ballet. The best result obtains when neither gets very far in time ahead of the other.

The whole esthetic of the movie derives from the fact that it is a photograph. Like all photography, it is naturally low in emotive appeal. We can stand a lot more blood and burst war-babies in a movie than we can in real life or on a stage. It is also low, for the same reasons, in human friendliness. The screen having no human odor at all, the friendliness is all out in the house, never between house and stage. Great actors get carried in triumph by their admirers; but movie stars, unless they are well protected, get torn to pieces by theirs, because these, not recognizing their idol in his human form and with unfamiliar odor, can only achieve a mystic communion with his image by destroying his flesh.

Its naturally low emotive appeal leads the film in three directions:

¶1. The depiction of natural scenery, as in documentaries.

¶2. Exploitation of the pathos of the human face, as in realistic fiction dramas with stars.

¶3. The flight into fantasy, as in comics and animated cartoons.

Conscious compensation by directors and cutters for photography's naturally low emotive appeal has produced a final product with a rather high emotive appeal, higher at least than is commonly obtainable by visual means.

The mobility of the camera (plus music) has produced a flexible and powerful art-form.

The same mobility is responsible for the movie's gravest inherent difficulty, the jerkiness of photographic narration. It would be absurd to keep the camera in one place all the time, as long as it can be so easily moved around. This constant shifting of the point of vision over an enormous variety of locales does make, however, for visual discontinuity. This discontinuity in turn is compensated for by an elaborate refinement of cutting. Cutting is the most admired technique in movie-making, the most difficult, and the most indispensable. When each scene's visual time-length is adjusted to a desired emotional impact, and the whole series of scenes bound together by musical continuity, you have a narrative that is not at all low in emotive power, even though the music for the most part at present is not very well adapted to its function.

Documentary subjects are the easiest kind of movie to write music for. The fantasy and the comedy are next. There exist a goodly number of excellent scores of all three kinds. I have never heard a satisfactory musical accompaniment to a spoken film drama. It was all very easy pinning music on to "silent" Westerns. Schubert's *Unfinished Symphony* and Debussy's *En Bateau* were adequate for anything. It is speech that has brought back the film's essential jerkiness, by interrupting the musical continuity.

For comics and documentaries and fantasies there is no grave trouble. All the composer needs to do is to put a continuous accompaniment of appropriate style under each sequence, making just enough timed illustrative "effects" to give everybody a slight shock at the major shifts in the narrative. Even if there is a speaker in the documentary, or some wisecracks to insert in the comic film, all is easy. The music can be stopped for short moments, its volume brought up or down, without its real progress being destroyed.

Before speech came in, the drama film presented the same problem as these others, the chief thing needed being musical continuity interspersed with timed "effects." What has not been satisfactorily solved yet is how to put music to the spoken drama film. How to make music that will be important enough to carry your big moments, and at the same time keep out of the way of the dialogue, is the problem. The future of the drama film depends on its solution. Otherwise, the movies will find themselves more and more limited to the making of documentaries, comedies, fantasies, and something like revues. The film drama cannot live without music, as stage drama can. And it is not getting much use right now out of the music it is living with.

The problem is not insoluble. It is really one of definition. Is the movie a visual art-form, or is it predominantly verbal? It is a visual art-form, of course; don't forget it is a photograph. Its humanly expressive range runs from pantomime to pageantry and back and not much further. But its intensity of expression within that range is greater than any hitherto available. The presentation in a theater of panoramic views of natural scenery and of gigantic enlargements (called "close-ups") of the human face is a possibility absolutely new to art, a possibility that is unique to the moving picture. Fantasy is not unique to the movies. The three-dimensional theater has its fantasy too, which is just as amusing as trick photography. Sleight-of-hand, for instance, is more convincing on a stage than on a screen. And the plastic possibilities of stage scenery, with its variety of stuffs and colors, its enormous range of luminosity, are greater than any plastic beauty the movies (even the colored movies) can touch. Human speech has more variety and power in a theater; music sounds better in a concert hall. Even radio-crooning (that close-up of the human voice) is more poignant without visual interference.

The animated cartoon, charming as it is, is not characteristically cinematographic. It is not even necessarily a photograph. It is a free-hand drawing, photography being merely its commonest projection method. Its relation to naturalistic cinematography is that of marionettes to the real-actor stage. Its whole esthetic, in fact, is that of the marionette theater, even to the use of strained vocalization. Its designers can produce masterpiece after masterpiece because they face no new esthetic problems.

Now any art-medium derives its own esthetic, as well as its power, from what is different about it, not from what is common to it and to other media. And what is specifically different about the movies from all other forms of theatrical entertainment is their ability to move our hearts by true representations of natural scenery and enlargements of the human face. If you will look back in your memory, or into the history books, you will find that at least nine-tenths of all the really famous and unforgettable films are films that were photographed mostly out of doors. And at least one of the most celebrated films in the world, Karl Dreyer's *La Passion de Jeanne d'Arc,* consists in large part of nothing but close-ups taken without make-up on anybody's face. There is no getting around it. The stage can beat the movies at painted scenery, at the plastic disposition of stuffs and color and light. The movies are inalienably (even in their most fantastic moments) tied up to some kind of naturalism. The two-dimensional monochrome screen (colored films are very little colored, and at best they derive more of their definition from chiaroscuro than from chromatics), the husky and booming voices, the shortness of scenes and consequent nervousness of even the best "continuity," these technically imposed distortions are as much stylization as anybody can stand. Further distortion of reality is unprofitable.

Plots need not necessarily be naturalistic. They can be as conventional, as romantic, as fantastic as you like; and the high-flown heroic is their oyster. The movies do not have (necessarily) plot trouble, and they are certainly not limited in subject-matter. They don't have necessarily acting trouble any more since a natural style of acting has been adopted. Everybody just acts as natural as he can, and he does that in houses and on grass and in front of landscapes that, if not always quite credible realistically, are invariably naturalistic in intention. What kind of trouble then do they have? They have stylistic trouble, trouble about words and music.

Words and music are an ancient marriage, the marriage whose eldest offspring are song and the opera. Words go all right with visual spectacles too; that makes the "legitimate" theater. Music and pantomime go fine; that is ballet. Music and photographs of real people or scenery are okay; that is the documentary film. Even music and printed words don't bother anybody; that's what you have at the beginnings of films in a section called Titles and Credits. The combination works one hundred per cent.

The aim and problem of the narrative film is nothing more or less than effective narration. Film narration is photographic narration, and in a photograph people are not convincing unless they look and act natural. If one wishes to look approximately natural, one had better not try to do too much explaining by gestures and facial pantomime, unless the limits of the medium impose that procedure. Before the days of the sound-film, that was the narrative method, that and occasional subtitles. Today it would be ridiculous not to profit by the added naturalism of speech, to pretend that stylized pantomimic explanations are obligatory, when everybody knows they are not. There are no films any more, excepting those of Charlie Chaplin, without some verbal text. That text is inevitably naturalistic too. It is frequently enlivened by wit and wisecrack, just as ordinary conversation is. Seldom is there fantasy or imagery, because these fall outside the naturalistic convention.

There are no films at all without music, which is more necessary even than the spoken word. It ties together the jerky narration (unless the composer of it makes the mistake of changing his music every time there is a change of scene, in which case he exaggerates the jerkiness). It produces quick, strong emotional reactions to reinforce the slow, weak ones that are all you get normally out of photography, out of anything visual, in fact. It also keeps the audience awake.

Photography, words, and music, how may these three elements be welded into an effective narration? You can't cut one out, because the movies cannot do without music, and it would be a little silly today to try to do without speech. Intoning the speech, as in opera, is entirely out of the question in any dramatic medium so completely tied up to naturalism. To put continuous music under the speech ("melodrama" is the technical term in music for this combination), is just as unsuitable to the naturalistic style as operatic *recitativo*. It is always corny and unconvincing unless the music has some naturalistic excuse for being there. To limit the subject-matter of films to stories in which music can be constantly present on naturalistic excuses would be to hamstring the art.

What is done is to open with music under the titles and credits, and then to alternate straight spoken passages with melodrama, with music, and with noises. Noises and music don't go badly together, curiously enough. There is a constant tendency to try to get the music and the words together also, to interpolate songs, because the fact is there isn't enough emotion-producing music in the fictional film today. And there is no musical continuity whatsoever. The documentaries use a continuous symphonic score and a fairly continuous speaker. The procedure works admirably; it does not make "melo-drama," because the music is accompanying the film (not the speaker), and the speaker is commenting the film (not the music). Music and speech exist in such spectacles at the same time; but they have no real connection, hence no serious interference.

There is a tendency in French movie-making to restore the continuous musical accompaniment, only interrupting it for important speeches, and cutting down the total amount of speech in the film to as small a proportion as possible. The system seems to work fairly well and would work even better if the composers who sign the scores could be given time to write their own music, all of it, and if a relatively stable dynamic level for sound-recording could be established. As it is, two hours of interesting music cannot be written and orchestrated in a week; and even if it could, the fading-away and loudening-up practice is musically unsatisfactory, though necessary for the sake of speech-clarity. It contradicts all dynamic variety that takes place at the music's source and makes the orchestra sound as if it were playing steadily fortissimo in a swell-box.

Even this excellent compromise system tends to limit the movies' subject-matter. It works best, really works only on plots that do not involve music. Because you can't have stage music and pit music both unless you have both a stage and a pit. All movie music comes from the same place, which is a loudspeaker somewhere near the screen. It is musically unclear to jump from commentary or background music to realistic music of any kind, and quite impossible to play the two off against each other antiphonally, unless the sounds come from different places. Using two loudspeakers would be useless, would merely destroy the illusion that any of the music at all comes from the screen. A sharply marked duality of musical style is the only feasible way of marking the transition from background music to realism; and that is a technique not easily applicable, unless one man really writes all the music, or unless two men really write it, casting themselves, as in a play, for their characteristic and personal qualities.

At present, the system of nearly continuous accompaniment, even if the music written for it were stylistically satisfactory, and even if the dynamic level of recording could be adjusted so that clear words and expressive music could cohabit without friction, is still rather insufficient for the narration of themes that involve much musical pageantry. It is over-sufficient and tiresome for any subject that deals familiarly with middle-class life. Music here gets in the way of naturalistic conversation and almost inevitably turns the story into melodrama. The

French system is at its best in dramas about life among the dregs and the outcasts or about life in exotic and lonely landscapes, life at sea or in unfrequented mountain-lands, deserts, places where people speak in dialect or with stylized accents and where everything is strange and violent and very very sad indeed. The removal from middle-class life that is inherent in such subjects makes it possible to use such a stylized convention as the nearly continuous musical accompaniment interspersed with picturesque speech.

The tie-up with middle-class naturalism, which seems to be ineluctable, has forced the American films to lean more and more on dialogue (for its naturalistic value) and less and less on music, thus sacrificing a great deal of music's emotional value and practically all of its value as continuity. This choice is not an improper one, but it has created a difficulty. Because the movies cannot live without lots and lots of music, and the insertion of lots and lots of music into naturalistic plays with middle-class dialogue is just now quite out of the question.

There are two ways currently employed of getting music back into the films. One is the interpolation into comic and light sentimental subjects of songs, dances, and night-club scenes, the presence of the latter being a firm convention in French films, where they correspond exactly to the ballet convention of French opera. Less universal, but not uncommon in America, is the insertion of jolly male choruses, military band music, arias from popular grand opera, and bits of such symphonic compositions as are familiar to radio audiences. All these are introduced with a naturalistic excuse of some kind; they are plot music and count as realistic detail, never as commentary or as continuity. They are music, however; and that is always a help. The other way is used for more serious and tragic themes. It demands the insertion, wherever possible, of commentary music. In order that this commentary be not too prominent, an attempt is made to write it in a neutral style. The result is not really neutral; let us call it, for lack of a better term, pseudo-neutral music. There are special composers in all the centers of film-manufacture who specialize in writing this. Do not despise them. They are experts and know exactly what they are doing. They are writing a musical journalese. Their aim is to make music that will be rich in harmonic texture and sumptuous in orchestration, but whose melodic material and expressive content will be so vague that nobody will notice it. Such music fulfills its minimum architectonic function of tying together the continuity at the points where it is absolutely necessary that that be done. It is also useful for underlining a bit of humor or a heart-throb and for creating fortissimo hubbub at the beginning and end of films, the time when people are changing their seats. It gives a general air of luxury by being there at all and by being orchestrated in the "picturesque" style of 1885, the style of Chabrier and of the early Richard Strauss. Its power of self-effacement is its real virtue. Few persons excepting those of predominantly auditive memory (and these rarely go to the movies) can ever remember anything about the music of serious drama films, even whether there was any or not. It is discreet; it is respectable; it comes and goes without being noticed. It carefully avoids ever making any underlining that might engage it subsequently to a close collaboration with the film story. It retires completely before the speaking voice, no matter how banal a remark that voice may be about to utter.

Neither of these ways is very satisfactory. The first turns everything into a musical comedy. The second is both architecturally and emotionally inefficient, because music can't be neutral and sumptuous at the same time. Not in this post-Wagnerian age. A really neutral music would be admirable, if it could be written. It would certainly provide a better contrasting background than the pseudo-neutral does for the insertion of stylized musical numbers. And it would serve as a sonorous foundation on which to erect musical climaxes that could support the big punches of the narrative in a pretty impressive way. It might even provide an approach to the central problem of words and music.

I do not know whether it is possible in this generation to develop a neutral music style. It existed in Europe from the Council of Trent to the middle of the eighteenth century. Its remains are buried in the pedagogical convention known as "strict" counterpoint. The basic rule of such music was the avoidance of any tonal formula that was at all noticeable or that was in any way specifically expressive. The German Romantic rule, our present tradition, is to make the music everywhere as noticeable and as expressive as possible. The international neo-classic style that I spoke about in another chapter was the product, in part, of an attempt to revive non-expressive counterpoint. Its practitioners thought to neutralize the expressive value of unresolved dissonances by making the employment of these obligatory and consistent. It cannot be said that strictly dissonant counterpoint, however useful as a pedagogic device, has provided the world with a stylistic discipline that quite fulfills the functions of the classic one. Rather it is a commentary on the more ancient rules that would make no sense at all to one who was not trained on these. The twelve-tone system of atonality is rather less neutral and more expressive than tonal counterpoint. If either of these modern conventions, or a revival of the classic one, should prove useful in the composition of film accompaniments, nobody would be more delighted than I; but so far I must say they have not done anyone much good. I must make an exception or two, for in French films I have occasionally heard an apt usage of dissonant counterpoint. Not for its expressive value; that is easy and no trouble. I mean as something approaching a really neutral background music, a *senza espressione* style that throws whatever is seen against it into high expressive relief.

It is really too bad the movies got born a century late. They would have served as an ideal dramatic medium for Richard Wagner. He, of course, is every movie-director's dream of a musician. He wouldn't have needed neutral music; he would have taken us all to Valhalla on continuous hubbub with intense expressivity everywhere. And no tommy-rot about pretending that the speaking voice is essential to realism or that middle-class life is in any way interesting. He would have placed the films, once and forever, on that high heroic plane that their colossal powers of visual depiction demand for them. History has willed it otherwise. Wagner did his heroic job, did it on the opera. It is too late now to do the same job on the movies, because the same battle can't ever be fought twice. His goddesses and heroes are fat theatrical screamers who stand around among cardboard rocks and wander through canvas forests. There is nothing naturalistic or credible about them; they are symbols embedded in concert music. But embedded they are; and Wagner is dead, and stage opera, too, very nearly. The films will have to go now in another direction and invent a new musical stylization. There is nothing to do about being born too late except to become a primitive.

The movie people are all very proud of their art's achievements. They think the movies are in every way just grand. Actors pretend otherwise, but they all think so too; and they are out for movie jobs to a man. Literary authors hate the movies with a violence, whether they work in the films or not. And composers of music, whether they work in films or not, are sad, unhappy, and nervous about them.

Any further progress esthetically in "pictures," as Hollywood so unpretentiously calls them, depends on first restoring the musical continuity. Emotional superpower must start from there. In order to restore musical continuity, either spoken dialogue must be thrown out or a new and practical working solution must be found for the words-and-music problem, a solution that will permit words and music either to let each other alone or to help each other out. At the moment, they are in each other's hair; and the low emotional tension that results is of very little support to the pallid and anæsthetic spectacle of narrative photography.

There has been a lot of talk about movie opera. Movie opera is a dead-end. At least it is if by movie opera you mean the screening of well-known stage operas. Original screen opera might be possible if it were called something else. But the word "opera" throws both directors and composers into nervous states that render them unfit for responsible art-work. No art form is so little understood or so stupidly practiced as the opera in this age of its decline. Even over the radio very little has been done except to broadcast repertory stage works, though heaven knows the opera as a musical form is just God's gift to the microphone. Writing contemporary operas for the crooning technique, how has everybody been so dumb as to miss it? I can only explain that miss on the ground that the word "opera" produces such sun-spots on the mental retina that once it is mentioned nobody can see anything but *Tristan* and *Faust* and *Il Trovatore*. I must say that making original screen opera will be no such child's play as making radio opera would be. But the movie banks have money, great big electrical money. There could be no real harm in their making half a dozen screen operas, if only to find out what not to do once the word "opera" shall have been got out of the way and it shall have become thenceforth possible to make serious musical fiction films.

MUSICAL THEATER

Opera is complete musical theater.

Musical theater is a collaboration of the verbal, the visual, and the tonal arts, usually with intention to instruct. The place of music in such a collaboration varies from epoch to epoch. A drum-roll to send up the curtain, accompaniments for dancing and acrobatics, an interpolated song here and there, the eternal off-stage trumpet calls, all these are incidental. It doesn't make much difference whether they are well-made or only fair. The quality of the music makes, however, a great deal of difference when that music is tied up to the dialogue. Such a tie-up is the specific characteristic of serious opera. Because of it, opera has the most ancient heritage of any theatrical form still practiced in the Western hemisphere.

The Greek tragic theater, like most religious ceremonies everywhere, was originally danced and sung. Even as late as Periclean times, when the poets had hogged the show for themselves, and the only religion left in it was a sort of civic morality, the mass recitations were still intoned and the chorus that intoned them pranced on in ceremonial quickstep. The Christians took over most of the Greek theatrical procedures for use in their ceremony of the Mass. This latter is a combination of tragic spectacle (the sacrifice of Our Lord is re-enacted) with practical magic, the elements of bread and wine being transubstantiated into the flesh of God and devoured beneficially by the initiates. Even the word *clericus* (or clergyman) means in late Latin an actor. To this day the Mass is danced and sung, which is to say that the text is intoned and all the movements are regulated. There is even provision for the interpolation of musical set-pieces, of choral entries, and of parades. The reprosodizing of the whole liturgical repertory to fit medieval Latin, which had become quite different in sound from classical Latin, and the composing of set-pieces to ornament this repertory occupied most of Europe's musical world for a thousand years, from the seventh to the seventeenth centuries.

The opera, as we know it, was invented in Florence in 1600, for the purpose of performing non-Christian (specifically, Greek mythological) tragic plays in Italian. The intention was anti-ecclesiastical. But the method employed for carrying out this intention was to take over (to take back rather) and to laicize all the musical procedures of the Church. Nothing could have been more intelligent. Because the formal procedures of music, as we have mentioned before, are not bound up with any ideological content. Also because these procedures were in this case exactly the musical procedures of the Greek tragic mythological theater, the art that it was desired to restore.

If musicians could ever get it through their heads again, after seventy-five years of having forgotten it, that the operatic form is nothing more or less than the form of the Christian Mass, as well as that of the Greek tragic theater, there would be far fewer unsuccessful operas produced in Europe and America every year. One single principle underlies the design, the structure of complete musical theater (whether you call that opera or music-drama). The basic routine of this, as of the Mass and of the ancient poetic stage, is intoned speech. Successive reformers of the opera (every time the opera gets domesticated to a new language it has within a century to be reformed) have varied the proportion of intoned dialogue, set-piece, and instrumental illustration; but they have never thrown out the central procedure, which is intoned dialogue. One might even say that the way to reform opera anywhere is to bring back the attention of composers to the basis of all opera, intoned speech.

You cannot write an opera, as you can a song, by making up a tune and then fitting words to it. You have to start from a text and stick to it. You must scan it correctly and set it to tunes convincingly. In the more vigorous operatic epochs singers even articulate it comprehensibly. Speech so scanned and set, if intoned with clear articulation, is both easier to understand and more expressive than speech that is not intoned; and it can be heard farther.

All the rest of an opera is just the icing on the cake. You can put in all the set-pieces you like and all the symphonic reinforcements. You can have the most beautiful scenery and clothes money can buy, or you can do without. You can regulate the singers' every movement, or you can let them wander around from bench to tree. You can add ballets, earthquakes, trained seals, trapeze acts, and an orchestra of a hundred and fifty musicians with sirens and cowbells. The more the merrier, because the opera is a complete art-form like the Mass, the Elizabethan theater, and the movies. An ideal opera contains one of everything. It is better than a circus because it can include a circus. Also, as at the circus, the audience is part of the show.

The opera has no time limits. It can last ten minutes or seven hours. It has few limits of subject-matter. Religious, moral, or even politically revolutionary themes that would be censored elsewhere so quickly you wouldn't know what had happened are accepted without shock at the opera (and understood). It has no limits about vocal or instrumental style. It is stylistically the freest of all the musical forms and the most varied. It can stand any amount of interpolated numbers, musical, scenic, or acrobatic. Its one limitation is the condition of its amplitude. It must always be a bunch of actors in character singing a play to an audience. Not singing a lullaby or a love song or a lament for virginity betrayed, but singing the remarks and speeches that make up a theatrical narrative. It is not a symphony with voices or an oratorio with scenery or an instrumental accompaniment to a pantomime, though at times it has tended to degenerate to all these.

Let us repeat it over and over. Basic opera is nothing more or less than an intoned play. Start from there, as the opera did and as every reformer of the opera has to, and you will arrive at complete musical theater. Start from anywhere else, and you arrive at incomplete musical forms and at very uninteresting theater.

* * *

I shall skip along briefly over the forms of incomplete musical theater such as Protestant church services, plays with incidental music, military ceremonies, and home weddings. The music to these is a sort of yardage that is cut to fit the cue-sheet and the colonel's taste. Putting incidental music to spoken plays does pose a structural problem of acoustic placement, any given bit of music becoming for the play scenery or property or framing, accordingly as the musicians executing it are placed in the wings or on the stage or in a pit. The combination of instrumental accompaniment with non-intoned speech, melodrama, adds tension to very short moments of a play; its abuse is a corny effect. A general rule of use to composers and play-directors is that music for plays works best if it makes some kind of continuity when played without any interruptions.

The most interesting (musically) of the incomplete musico-theatrical forms is the ballet. The great secret about that, the open secret that composers tend to forget, is that ballet music is, believe it or not, dance music. Its first function is muscular, helping the dancers move themselves around. It is a whip, not a musical meditation. Its rhythmic substructure is essentially percussive, because only beat music moves muscles. Music that has a quantitative rhythmic substructure without percussive thumps, the kind of music that comes from pipe organs, merry-go-rounds, player-pianos, harpsichords, and really hot swing orchestras, is not very good for provoking large muscular movements. The jitterbug twitch is about as far as any of these go.

Ballet music is not limited to percussive music. It is extraordinary the amount of static tone-pattern that can be got into it if you play this off frankly against the muscle-music. Stylistically the ballet is a rich and ample music-form, capable of almost as great variety of expression as the opera itself. I call it incomplete, compared to the latter, because of its lack of human song. Efforts have been made to add singing to the ballet; but these have not been very often successful, because singing is a more powerful medium of expression than bodily movements are. Every time you put vocalism alongside of dancing, the dancing has a way of becoming invisible. And the addition of dancing to a primarily vocal manifestation like opera, though a bit of ballet is pleasant enough as an interlude in a long vocal evening, certainly tends to diminish the intensity of the story-telling at that point. Intoned speech, however, is a strong enough foundation to support any and every kind of ornamental addition that might possibly enrich the whole spectacle, whereas pantomime and bodily prowess, no matter how breath-taking, are not a strong medium of expression. They are always tending (this is history) to lose what expression they have and to become just empty conventions. The reformers of the ballet are invariably preoccupied with trying to make stage dancing mean anything at all.

Like the movies, the ballet is a visual spectacle; and like all things visual, it is emotionally frigid. It needs music for continuity and for emotional intensity. Mixing it with opera is always exciting, though sometimes a little precarious. It is advantageous to the opera to have the movements of the actors regulated by an experienced choreographer. Even naturalistic opera profits by such collaboration. But that does not make a ballet of the opera any more than having a high-class artist design scenery and costumes will turn the visible stage into an oil painting.

Ballet is the expression of human sentiments by means of the muscular members. Its higher schools are opposed to any facial pantomime whatsoever, because facial expressions of any intensity tend to weaken the force of the body's all-over expressiveness, to personalize a highly impersonal art. Ballet is much enhanced, however, by scenery and clothes. The addition to one long-distance visual effect, which is dancing, of another, appropriate decoration, doubles the power of the whole visual spectacle. Just as the addition of music, which is auditory, to declamation, which is also auditory, makes the opera the most powerful auditory expression there is. Putting music under dancing is fine, because dancing needs it. Putting vocalism and dancing together is rarely effective for more than a short moment. Alternating dancing with vocalism, on the other hand, is completely satisfactory and charming, whether that is done with the grandeur of Lully's and of Rameau's sumptuous ballet-operas or with the unpretentious and simple good-humor of that ever-popular number, the song-and-dance.

HOW TO WRITE A PIECE

CONCERT MUSIC

The concert is the purest form of music, though not the most complete. It is not a complete art-form, like the opera, because it is limited to music. It is even a less complete musical form than the opera, because its repertory is limited formally to pieces of a certain length and stylistically to those of a certain respectability. It is music, only music, and (theoretically) high-class music. It tells no story, serves no didactic purpose; and the only spectacle it offers is that of men at work.

It is a very intense little affair. It is the islanders' form of the Communion of Saints, a communication from musicians to the "musical." For outsiders it is either a social ceremony or a place to let the mind wander pleasantly. For the unmusical this mind-wandering consists chiefly of sexual stirrings and memories of natural scenery. The musically sensitive find sometimes that music fecundates all sorts of thought. The meditative possibilities of musical listening are of the highest psychological value; I would not deny them to anyone. Only I insist that persons in a concert hall who are doing their own private business, whether that business is looking impressively social or thinking about love or laying plans for tomorrow, are not necessarily receiving any musical communication, though sometimes they may be doing that too.

In general, the best receivers of musical communications are persons of some active musical experience, persons whose visceral reactions are sensitive to auditory stimuli and who have some acquaintance from practice with the musical conventions by which these reactions are habitually stimulated. Such people are said to "understand" music. You can teach musical analysis to the tone-deaf; but you cannot make them understand music. Because the first condition of musical understanding is some visceral responsiveness to sound, and that you simply have from birth or you haven't. The blood-flow, the liver, the ductless glands, the digestive juices are entirely beyond voluntary control or training. If your reactions to musical sounds are sufficient to make concentration on these a pleasant activity, then of course the conscious mind comes into the process, comes in just as automatically as the viscera do, though a little later in time.

The process of intellection about music that all musical persons go through as they hear music is not a process of describing to oneself verbally the music's meaning. It is a process of being aware sensuously of certain visceral changes and clearly, auditively, separately aware of the sounds that provoke them. This dual process is quite facile when the music is familiar; hence everybody loves old music. With new music everything is much more difficult. Both the visceral reactions and the auditive experience that provokes them must be tasted, very much as one tastes strange foods. One isn't always sure right off whether one is going to "like" them or not. This process of discrimination is an intellectual (though largely unconscious) exercise of personal taste. Taste is knowing what you don't like. It is the knowledge of what you personally cannot take, what you must keep your viscera from getting too intimate with till your mind gets used to the novelty and you can accept the whole thing into your repertory of digestible experiences.

Music that is novel in stylistic orientation, that impinges strangely on the musical ear, provokes violent demonstrations of acceptance and refusal. The broader the musical experience of the listeners present, the more violent the public demonstration. In the great musical centers there is not seldom a physical brawl. The following principles govern taste judgments:

¶1. The degree of any group reaction, favorable or unfavorable, is more significant than its direction. Its strength is roughly proportional, over a certain period of time, to the expressive power of the work. An inexpressive work creates little disturbance.

¶2. The direction of the judgment, for or against, of each separate listener is influenced by his financial interest.

Teachers resist anything which contradicts what they

have been telling their students or that threatens to put them in a position of ignorance in front of these. They don't like envisaging a loss of student prestige, because that loss means eventually a money loss.

Composers resist anything that threatens competition. If a work is in similar vein to some piece of theirs, but more expressive, they hate it. Anything in similar vein, but definitely less expressive, they love. About anything quite different from their own work, they are benevolent but fairly silent, because they are already planning a little theft or two of a device.

Persons who have some musical experience but who are not making any money to speak of out of it have a relatively disinterested musical taste; and since the human mind always loves a little bit of change, these persons are eager to understand and to accept. They constitute an advance guard for the absorption of new music.

In places where musical sensitivity is so great and musical experience so general that everybody likes nearly everything, the musical tradition is said to be "decadent." Enormous quantities of music are consumed, but none of it means much. It is elaborate in construction and texture, low in expressive content. In such places and at such times, the consumption of old music (music already absorbed by the profession long ago) reaches a degree of popularity equal to (and in the final stages of decay superior to) that of new music. Nobody cares about either style or design. The music world is like a drunkard who has no digestion. He can't eat. He can only swallow more and more alcohol, any alcohol, till he falls down one day in *delirium tremens.* All the categories get confused and the values falsified. The opera becomes instrumental and unsingable. Ballet, instead of standing on its toes and holding its stomach in, which is where the ballet belongs if it expects to execute any variety of large free movements, stands flat on its feet and sticks its stomach out, waves an arm, and loses its balance. Song-and-dance folklore is imported from foreign climes, and the concert world is taken over by incompetent soloists and by overcompetent orchestral conductors who streamline the already predigested classics to a point of suavity where they go through everybody like a dose of castor oil.

As you see, this description fits quite accurately Germany for the past seventy-five years and not too badly the whole international music world. The concert tradition everywhere is esthetically in a bad way; it can't keep its eyes off the past. The opera too looks pretty sick as contemporary art. None of this is anybody's fault. Civilizations rise and civilizations die, and they usually overlap by several centuries. I am not writing a history of musical civilizations; I am describing the state of music. And the state of art-music everywhere in the West

(I don't know Asia or Islam) is unquestionably more than a little bit decadent.

In the Americas popular music is very healthy indeed, though this does not mean that the Great Tradition is about to be taken over by the swing cats. Maybe it is and maybe it isn't; I wouldn't know. It does mean, though, that there is more good music around than ever gets through to the opera houses and to the trusts of concert management. These last, with their one thousand symphony orchestras around the world, however much invested capital they may represent, have about the same relation to today's creative activity in music that the museums (including the so-called "modern" museums) have to contemporary painting. There are musical activities of a popular nature and others of a recondite intellectual nature (far from popular) that enclose the nuclei of the next musical civilization. Without going into the ways and means of forcing that, which would be another book and which could not possibly represent anything but wishful prophecy on my part, it is still easy to see, none the less, that the official, the rich opera-and-concert world of today is the resplendent tail-end of a comet that has already gone around the corner.

The principal "form," design, or pattern involved in concert music is the concert itself, which is a sort of musical meal, proceeding, as meals do, from heavy to light in digestibility. A good deal of ingenuity and taste goes into the designing of this meal, into the fitting of admissible pieces together so that they fall within a given time limit (a quite strict one in most cases) in mutually advantageous juxtaposition. But program-making is not musical composition any more than hanging a show of pictures is oil painting. And the analysis of concert pieces shows that they nearly all have some kind of a plan. If enough pieces have the same kind of plan, that plan gets called a "form."

As I have said before, I am not very fond of the word. I do not think that sonatas and rondos and such are musical forms. I think they are merely rhetorical devices. I except the dance meters, which have a real metrical convention, and the round, the canon, the fugal exposition, which follow a tonal one. In any case, information about them is not lacking. You can read them up in the Appreciation books (mostly misinforming, I admit) or in the professional text-books of musical analysis (which are better). You can learn about them all in half an hour.

Such matters have a practical interest for persons who write music and a lesser but also certain interest for executants. Detailed knowledge about them is just as useful to the layman as a receipt for angel-food cake would be to an unmarried dock-hand. The only real problem involved in musical rhetoric is how to make a piece last some time without getting vague. It must hold the auditor's interest without confusing him. And it must do this, as the movies do it, by continuity.

Music's first dimension is length, a length of time. An important expression of any emotional thing (and music is certainly not much but emotional) requires time. Short expressions can be intense, but only long ones can be ample. Coherence, in any piece of time, requires a continuity plan. Music made to be heard must be very simple indeed, must repeat its chief material over and over. It is not like a book, where the reader can stop and turn back and get the plot straightened out if he forgets. It must have such a simple layout or build-up that nobody can fail to follow it.

If you are still interested in how this gets accomplished, go to the books. The commoner layouts are all listed there and can be learned very quickly. What is important, however, about the structure of a piece is not what layout is used and with or without what traditional observances, but whether an average musician can understand the music. Can he memorize it well enough in a week to communicate it to another average musician? This is where the well-known formal layouts come in. Classifying the layout is the first step in musical analysis. And musical analysis is (usually) the first step in memorizing. That is about its last utility too, I suspect, that it is an aid to memory. Indeed it is a great aid, and the ability to practice it is indispensable to active musicians. I doubt that it is of much value to passive listeners.

Now don't imagine for a moment that I despise musical passivity. No sight is more pleasing to a composer that that of a houseful of completely quiet people listening to some work of his being executed. If any of them are listening analytically, that is perfectly all right by me. The analysis of my music has never lost me a customer yet. But for those who enjoy taking music passively (which is the only way most people not musicians can take it at all), I've an idea the process works better when their minds are really passive. Both to musicians and to laymen I recommend the mastery of non-cerebral receptivity. You can take the piece apart at some other time, at a time when time itself is not of the essence. A run-through performance is for nourishment, not analysis. Let the music quicken your pulse and thicken your blood and turn over your liver and digest your food. Let your mind alone and don't worry about the second theme. Try the music on and see if it fits as is. You'll find yourself remembering it much better than if you tried to analyze it and in doing so missed half of it.

In my student days I used to go to the Boston Symphony concerts every week. I found that if I arrived with my conscious mind already at a certain degree of musical saturation, as I often did, the only way I could understand anything the orchestra played was by not listening consciously at all. I would read the program. The Boston Symphony program in those days was a whole book, full of historic information and source-quotations. There was enough to last a good two hours; and all very diverting it was too, and cultural and harmless. The music provided just enough slight-annoyance value (like railway riding noises) to keep my attention on the reading. And the reading provided a subject for conscious attention to play with that enabled me really to hear the music. Occasionally the music would pull me away from the book and make me listen to it all over me. More often I just read on, paying no attention to the music, and of course never missing a note of it. Later I usually remembered it all, remembered it a great deal better than I should have if I had gone to sleep trying to listen and to analyze.

Musical analysis is a musician's job, just as chemical analysis is a chemist's. A concert is not, after all, even in its most recondite and tendentious examples, a display of musical specimens. A music library is that, if you must; but a concert is a meal. It is a feast, a ham sandwich, a chocolate sundae, nourishment to be absorbed with pleasure and digested by unconscious processes. The body has more use for music than the mind has. Take it or leave it according to the body's taste. Express your pleasure by applause, your displeasure by whistling and stamping, or by not coming again. If you live in a social group that cultivates musical opinions, tell your friends exactly what you thought of a piece afterwards, if you thought about it afterwards at all. If not, say so. And if your responses to the tonal art are low, then why be bothered with concerts anyway? There are always prize fights and tennis matches and matinées and dancing and eating and taking a walk and having a baby and quarreling and reading a book and getting tight. You are wasting good time to submit yourself to music unless you understand it viscerally. If you do understand it that way, then serious musical study and listening will be profitable to you. Otherwise I am afraid they will just confuse the mind with culture. I respect and admire sincerely persons who admit they are not interested in music.

Literally thousands of people go to concerts who are not responsive to music. Maybe I underestimate the musicality of opera and concert subscribers. I hope so, but I am not convinced. The audiences at cheap popular orchestral concerts are just like audiences everywhere, and I understand their responses without any trouble. The well-to-do (usually female) subscriber, I do not really believe to be musically alert. I am convinced, though I can't prove it, that about one-fourth of the persons who go regularly to high-class concerts have no interest in what they hear and don't remember what they hear, that they are present from quite other than musical motivations, and that they know in advance they are going to be bored. There is, of course, no way of verifying my proportion. It might be much lower or much higher.

In any case, there are plenty of bored ones. Everybody knows that. The more expensive the seats the more boredom there is, as a general rule. These bored ones swell the receipts, of course; but they lower the potential of communication. If they are too numerous, they act as insulators and there is no communication. The receiving potential of audiences runs approximately as follows:

The most sensitive is the hand-picked invited audience, exception being made for invited radio audiences, which consist of company stooges.

Next come the audiences for chamber-music concerts. These contain a high proportion of professional musicians and almost no outsiders.

Audiences at concerts of pianists and solo violinists react rather strongly, on account of the large number of persons present who know from practice the technique and repertory of these instruments.

The same applies in a lesser degree to audiences for vocal soloists and for choral groups. Applause may run high; that means very little. In fact, the lower the culture-level of any audience, the greater that audience's enthusiasm for what it can understand.

The symphony addicts are, it seems to me, not very receptive, though the poor things haven't had much chance to receive, I must say, since world repertory got standardized. The resident orchestras suffer too from the social glamour brought to them by their rich founders and their pseudo-philanthropic trustees. This prestige brings in large numbers of impressive box-holders and subscribers whose active musical experience is low compared to their passive experience. (They have been to everything.) Even among the musical persons present, there are many who have only the vaguest acquaintance with orchestral instruments. Musical communication to these persons is a little incomplete. To the others it is practically nil. I know ladies who have been going to symphony concerts since childhood and who are lucky at sixty if they can recognize eight pieces out of the about fifty that make up the permanent repertory. These women are not stupid; they are just not very musical. They go to symphony concerts for reasons. I don't mean always social reasons, either, although a great many people do go to symphony concerts to be seen, just the way they used to go to the opera. What they like about orchestral concerts mostly, I think, is (a) the conductor and (b) the resemblance of the musical execution's superfinish to that of the other streamlined luxury-products with which their lives are surrounded. They feel at home, as if they were among "nice things," and as if the Revolution (or whatever it is that troubles rich people's minds) were far, far away. I don't think they are entirely bored. But I have always found them musically not very discriminating.

The invited radio audience is sterile. Practically no communication takes place at all; it isn't allowed to. The audience is only there to keep the players from getting bored or from getting mike-fright. It is an unpaid stooge. Applause is only allowed on cue; an adverse reaction of any kind is strictly forbidden, would be cut off the air if it took place.

Don't try to tell me any communication is going on, either, from the broadcasting room to the fireside listener. The listener begins by receiving a communication; but as soon as he learns that his reactions are producing no counter-reaction, he stops reacting. The radio concert is a good occasion to practice at home non-cerebral listening, to hear music while reading a book or washing dishes. Otherwise, the whole effect of radio concerts is dogmatic and scholastic, due to the absence of give-and-take. The best ones are those broadcast from public halls, because there you get a bit of the artist-audience interaction. Even in these broadcasts, there is always a speaker who manages to give you the idea that he is a hired salesman trying to make you sign something about the classics. It is pathetic the way he pleads with us to please believe everything in music is just hunky-dory, when we all know perfectly well that that last piece was a turkey and the house a frigidaire.

The Women's Club concert, the School-and-College-Trade concert and the Modern Music concert are special formulas. Each has its own repertory and its style of rendition, determined by the character of its highly stylized public. This public has in each case a moderately intense but highly stylized receptivity. Its audience reactions to any piece vary little all over the world.

The club formula aims to charm rather than to instruct. It avoids both novelty and brilliance. The school-and-college formula aims to instruct, and to this end seeks the shock value of novel or rare repertories rather than the stylish execution of chestnuts. A too-sophisticated execution is rather frowned on, in fact, and rightly, for it would get in the way of musical communication. A neutral rendition is better for unfamiliar music than a misapplication of some colorful technique to the wrong work or period.

Modern Music programs are made up almost exclusively of first performances in the locality. The audience is restless, picturesquely dressed, intellectually distinguished, and definitely international-minded. At least two-thirds of it is made up of practicing musicians and other artistic professionals. It is a hot-bed of musical politics. Critical acrimony runs high.

From 1919 to 1929, these concerts represented the international front-line trench of the newer new music. Since that time new music, at least the music of the younger composers, has appeared more often in the theater, in the films, on the radio, and in private concerts. Because the societies for the promulgation of modern music (those that still exist) have come to represent a vested interest, the right of the previous decade's bright young men to censor this decade's production and to decide on its worthiness for performance beside their own. This decade's bright young men have, in consequence, adapted their music to commercial and private outlets, to the rather considerable advantage of both music and its commerce. The next decade's young (they are turning up in some abundance of late) show signs of inventing a less internationalist form of new-music concert and naturally of running it themselves, as the young people of the 1920's did. They will not do much about concerts of any kind, however, as long as there is any chance of their getting into commerce with applied music.

Just a word about the stylistic conventions of the Modern Music societies. An ideal program for any concert would be made up of pieces that were never intended to be played in concert. Such a program would have a rich variety of subject-matter and of musical style. As soon as a series of concerts, however, becomes a production outlet, composers start producing for that outlet. The concerts of any Modern Music society are primarily an outlet for the group of composers who constitute its program-committee. Any piece is refused that is more spectacular in subject-matter or treatment than the pieces it must appear beside, or sufficiently less spectacular so that somebody's music (you never know whose) might be made to sound a little silly. Let us suppose a young man writes a piece for private reasons, and that some society produces it and no great harm is done. He is promptly asked to submit another and encouraged to write something especially for the society. That means he must keep in mind, while writing his piece, its relation to the kind of thing that it is likely to have to appear on the program with. If he transgresses that consideration, his piece will not be performed. A piece will be performed by somebody who has kept the unspoken rule and the unannounced pieces in mind.

The esthetic problem thus posed for all composers who do not have a society of their own, but who would like a little outlet all the same, is that of writing music that will not seriously endanger the success of certain other music. Professional advantages are offered as reward for happy solutions. The result of it all, in the 1920's, was the creation of an international school that tended more and more to become neutral in subject-matter, conformist in style. Everybody wonders why the modern symphonies played at endowed symphony concerts sound tame. That is the condition of their being played at all, that they shall not seriously compete with standardized repertory. People wonder too why so much of modern music, though it sounds violent, seems to say nothing comprehensible. That, my children, was the condition of its being played in the concerts of the international Modern Music ring. The dissonant contrapuntal was the only style admitted. It naturally got more and more so and just as naturally less and less expressive. I shall never forget the scandal in the world of modernist music that greeted the appearance of Sauguet's ballet *La Chatte* and of my own opera *Four Saints in Three Acts*. After twenty years of everybody's trying to make music just a little bit louder and more unmitigated and more complex than anybody else's, naturally everybody's sounded pretty much alike. When we went them one better and made music that was simple, melodic, and harmonious, the fury of the vested interests of modernism flared up like a gas-tank. That fury still burns in academic places. In my own case it is strongest where I was educated. At Harvard and among the Nadia Boulanger coterie in Paris I am considered a graceless whelp, a frivolous mountebank, an unfair competitor, and a dangerous character.

CHAPTER ELEVEN

BACK TO THE WOMB, JAMES, or

How modern music gets that way

SO FAR I have taken for granted the common assumption of our time that the Arts are a little different from all other skills and from all other branches of knowledge. This assumption is an ancient one, although the definition of what is and what isn't an art has varied greatly from age to age. The modern conception is derived from the Greek mythological metaphor of the Muses, to which has been added, as a divine afflatus informing them all, the Hebraic and Christian concept of a Holy Ghost "who speaks by the prophets."

The three springs that issue from the slopes of Mount Helicon were in Bœotian times supposed to be presided over by three earth deities known as Meditation, Memory, and Song. By Athenian times these three had got subdivided into nine. They were, if I may remind you:

Music, which included the science of acoustics,
Astronomy, which included the science of numerology,
Dancing, both religious and theatrical,
History, whether that was written in verse or not,
Comedy,
Tragedy,
Elegy,
Lyric Poetry, and
Oratory, which included the recital of heroic poetry.

Please notice the enormous preponderance in this list of what we should call Literature and the complete absence of the visual arts.

The medieval schools used a different list. They included under the one word *ars,* which meant craft, the techniques of all the factibilia, of everything that could be made, from cake to sarcophagi. But they recognized seven major branches of learning, namely: Grammar, Logic, Rhetoric, Arithmetic, Geometry, Music, and Astronomy.

The division of all the techniques into Liberal Arts, or those which deal in knowledge rather than skill of hand, Mechanical Arts, which is what we would mean by the *crafts,* and the Beautiful Arts, seven of them in number, is a Renaissance conception. The Beautiful Arts turn out to be our old Greek friends, minus History and Astronomy, and with all the visual or plastic techniques added. That is to say, they are Music, Painting, Sculpture, Architecture, Poetry, Eloquence, and Choreography.

The modern world has a tendency to accept this list, but to group the Seven Arts into three main categories: the visual, commonly called plastic; the verbal, generally denominated as Literature; and the auditive, which means music and all of its collaborative manifestations. There is another modern tendency that wishes to separate all intellectual achievement into the imaginative (laymen call this "creative") and the scholarly branches. This is just another way of saying the Beautiful Arts versus the Liberal and gets us nowhere.

I have often wondered if there were any necessary connection or similarity at all between the visual arts, the verbal, and the auditive, beyond the fact that their practitioners often live in the same neighborhoods when they are young and poor and have to, and consequently are all more or less acquainted. Certainly the ability to consume with discrimination art-products of all three kinds is practically never encountered in any one customer. The paint-lovers are highly indifferent to music, and heaven knows the music-lovers' taste in the plastic arts is elementary. However that may be, the concept of "the Arts" is embedded in our thought and language. About all we can do with it is to relist the techniques, to regroup them along pedagogical, psychological, technical, moralistic, or economic lines. I have myself a little idea that it might be useful to envisage the art techniques according to their working-methods, as solitary versus collective.

I have avoided so far, wherever possible, using the word "collective," because it has been so bound up of late with partisan politics and class warfare that I have preferred to use the word "collaborative," which is much less emotion-producing, to describe art-work that is executed by some person not the designer of it. I find at this point that I need both words, one to describe collaborative design, like the writing of operas, ballets, theatrical works in general, and the planning of architecture, and the other to describe the execution of any design by skilled workmen, whether that design is a one-man effort or a three-man collaboration. So if you don't mind and if you will kindly, before going on, take time out to pacify whatever hopes and fears that word may rouse in your breast, we will hereinafter refer to all art-work as "collective" art which is executed by craftsmen from a design. That design may have been made by solitary or by collaborative methods; if it is executed by other persons than the designer, the work is some kind of a collective product.

It is probably the tendency of all skills to remain collective as long as their techniques are expanding and to become personal, private, solitary, to contract, in short, when no means for further technical expansion are available. Painting and Poetry were collective arts once. Sculpture and Architecture are still, also Choreography and Eloquence (if that means prepared declamation). And so is Music.

I mentioned in the very beginning of this book that there was no such thing, in my opinion, as the Modern Spirit, that there were only some modern techniques. Yet all laymen are convinced that modern poetry, modern painting, and modern music have something in common. What modern painting and modern poetry have in common is the discovery of the mental discipline of dissociation. That is the characteristic thought-device to which we owe both Cubist painting and Miss G. Stein's poetic writings.

For artists the discipline of dissociation is a discipline in spontaneity. For scientists it is a discipline in avoiding spontaneity, which would mean the acceptance of common-sense judgments and axioms. The dissociation of image from design in painting, the simultaneous representation of multiple sight-lines, the juggling of word sounds and the jumbling of word meanings in poetry, are spontaneous, subjective dissociations; the only verification possible of their validity as communication is the equally spontaneous (but collective and hence authoritative) judgment of the whole body of persons who have taste and some training for the reception of beauty visual and linguistic.

This beauty being made all by one man, one would naturally expect criticism to play a large rôle in its reception. Curiously enough, it doesn't. Painting is practically without criticism today and poetry very nearly. Because you cannot criticize without standards, and there are no standards possible for evaluating one-man beauty. There is only voting, yes or no. Criticism of the collective arts is very vigorous, however; and it collaborates in their dissemination and absorption, even in their manufacture.

The discipline of spontaneity has not been very fecund for sculpture, acting, or oratory. It has not worked too badly in architecture. It has not been possible to apply it to music at all in any new way, because music is the one art where it has already been practiced, knowingly and systematically, for centuries. Modernism in music exists all right, or used to; but it has nothing whatsoever to do with modernism in painting or in poetry. Such modernism as exists in musical art (let us be perfectly clear about this) is not so much a matter of any recent vogue for discord, or of any new acoustical discoveries, or of any very great amplification of harmonic resources, as it is a general loosening up, a progressive efflorescence in decay, of the conventions of musical expression. It has been going on since the end of the eighteenth century.

Let me go back a little in history. Every art has its high-brow and its low-brow manifestations, its official canon and its folklore. During Byzantine and medieval times painting and sculpture and architecture, all the visuals, were subject on the one hand to a set of esoteric rules called the Principles of Design, largely derived, if I mistake not, from astrology and from mystical numerology; and on the other to the pressure of popular taste, which is always utilitarian, sentimental, and humanistic. From the Italian Renaissance to the French Revolution all three arts became increasingly humanistic, and the esoteric laws of Design fell into progressive disrepute. By the end of the eighteenth century improvisational one-man easel-painting in oil was about all the painting there was. Like that of all one-man jobs, its business was to express private and personal views of subject-matter, to show how anything looks to one man's Seeing Eye. During the nineteenth century, though certain discoveries were made about light and its depiction by color, design just didn't interest anybody.

In the early years of the twentieth century, Paris was the center of an attempt to invigorate all the visual arts by reintroducing design as a major element in pictorial composition. I do not think this motivation was entirely conscious on anybody's part. I think the more dominant conscious desire was to bring painting intellectually up-to-date and thus to please a larger and less hard-boiled public than the nineteenth-century capitalists, a public disillusioned about money and politics, that had read all the socialist and scientific writers and was very nervous about slum conditions. It is not my purpose to recount in detail how a proletarian, a populistic movement was turned into the aristocratic and recondite Cubist revolution or to pronounce on the ultimate success of this last, because the painting-war it started is far from over. I only want to point out by all this hasty history that the art of oil-painting had gone so far solitary, private, and personal by 1900 that it took a revolution within the profession to get it admitted that esoteric matters were involved at all in the painting of easel-pictures. The painting of these is still practiced, of course, as a one-man job, subject to no collective criticism any more valid than market quotations. As a matter of fact, in Paris today a painter is not even judged by his peers; he is judged by poets, political philosophers, and dressmakers (under dressmakers include the periodical organs of women's wear). Pablo Picasso cannot influence the market price of any painter's work. Miss Gertrude Stein, André Breton, and *Vogue* magazine can. The whole profession of painting is anarchy. The painters, as a group, are as devoid of organization as the visible world they depict.

They are an infinite multiplicity of nice little men, all got up in trick hair-cuts and coquettish tweeds, parading their imaginary sex-appeal around with a naïve persistence only equaled by the naïve persistence with which they produce by the most advanced methods of automatic workmanship picture after picture almost any one of which might have been painted by almost any one of them.

The history of poetry is essentially the same, though the timing of the periods is all different. It is a history of progressive shrinking in both length and subject-matter since the art began to work on a solitary production-system, since it gave up the stage, in fact.

Solitary art-workers, it would seem, tend to produce smallish works not differing very much from one artist to another in either style or subject-matter. They have the old trouble about solo improvisation, which is practically always conformist and corny. A prepared declamation of poetry can be pretty fine; improvised oratory is mostly silly. Solo improvisation is the triumph of the one-job man on the one-man job. Collective improvisation is a very different thing. Improvisational one-man easel-painting is sold to millionaires as high art. It is mostly today just the folklore of intellectual Paris. Jazz and swing music are sold to everybody as the folklore of dumb-bell America. They have lately, however, through the practice of collective improvisation, come to be among the most varied, elaborate, and expressive of modern art products, and of them all, scarcely excepting the movies, the most widely disseminated.

The question of how modern painting got to be that way, at what point in time it ceased to be designed objective depiction and became personal depiction, bothers the painters themselves a good deal, though the customers don't seem to care much. They use it as decoration anyway. The question of how Romantic music grew into Modern music bothers everybody but musicians. Because musicians know something that the outsiders, flustered and fascinated by the painting boom and the physical science boom and the psychoanalytic-introspection boom, don't know at all. They know, they still know, how to combine humane expression, a popular, a low-brow thing and always a non-canonical thing, with auditive beauty, which is a set of ancient and esoteric techniques, the employment of which to accomplish sentimental and expressive purposes has been practiced by the musical profession for centuries. And the essential device in that practice is exactly what seems so novel and exciting to painters, the mental disciplines of dissociation and spontaneity.

Let me elucidate. The basic material of Western music, our diatonic scale, is of strictly numerological origin. The only tones admitted in it are those bearing certain simple arithmetical ratios (expressible either by the length of a vibrating body or by the number of air-vibrations produced by whatever means per second) to a basic tone whose frequency of similar vibrations is represented by the number one. The tones so derived constitute our gamut, our whole palette of tonal resource. This gamut is of Greek origin. It has been subject to successive adjustments and amplifications to make it concord with acoustical facts (notably with the whole natural harmonic series), the last of these adjustments being the adoption about two hundred years ago of a falsified, or "tempered," scale for keyed instruments. Other races in other climes use other scales or gamuts. None of them, including ours, concords entirely with the harmonic series or with mathematical acoustics. But for good or ill, ours is ours, and the tonal patterns we write down are written in that alphabet.

When a tonal pattern of any kind is combined with a metrical one, the result is correctly called a musical "composition" whether it expresses anything very definite or not. The pattern of a musical composition may be strictly numerological, esoteric, and magical. (Enormous quantities of such music were written during the Middle Ages and still are.) Its first effect on him who executes and on him who listens is none the less a muscular and a viscero-emotional, a personal one. The conscious mind can be made to transfer the muscular and viscero-emotional effects to impersonal verbo-intellectual conceptions by combining music with verbal texts or with social observances of recognizable meaning, such as love-making, story-telling, marching, or dancing.

Among the Greeks, the Chinese, the Hindoos, and the Latin peoples, music was and is predominantly restricted to usages of the latter nature, to matters of which the social significance can be somewhat controlled. The Africans, the Arabs, and the Germanic races are given to the practice of a more directly physical music, which, instead of producing emotional intensifications of socially permissible ideas and actions, produces ecstatic states of a completely physical, non-intellectual, even anti-social character. In the case of the negroes and Arabs, these ecstasies are expressed muscularly by jerks and catalepsies. Consciousness and attention are as if absent. The usual antidote for over-indulgence in such ecstasies is sexual intercourse. In the case of the Germanic races, the ecstasy takes the form of a muscular relaxation combined with concentration of mental attention on the obscurest of all our sensations, the visceral ones. The antidote for over-indulgence in this practice is eating.

Children who have, by accident or atavism, a facility for remembering and reproducing both tonal and metrical patterns are said to have musical talent. This facility, like all talents, either grows or diminishes. To grow it must be exercised in musical execution. Listening to music will not satisfy musical tendencies or develop musical talent any more than watching sports will satisfy the play-instinct or develop muscles. A person so trained (and training has to include experience) is said to be a musician. Persons whose training and experience are perfectly real, but insufficient to meet the professional competition of the day, are commonly referred to as "musical." Persons who are without experience in musical execution are properly called "not musical." These persons may even show a history of extended lesson-taking. They are unmusical all the same if they cannot separate a musical pattern from its muscular and viscero-emotional effects and remember the musical pattern.

Instrumental training, musical analysis, and the practice of musical composition are based on a complete dissociation of all the elements, not only of the elements of pattern from one another, but of pattern itself from expression. Workers in the verbal and the visual arts do not go, I think, so far in this dissociative breakdown of technique as musicians do. For us melody is one thing. Counterpoint is another. Harmony is still another. In any melodic line the tonal pattern is separable from the rhythmic. In any harmonic progression the chord-series is separable from the voice leading, or melodic structure, of the instrumental parts combining to form that harmony. On the instruments that can play several tones at once, there is not necessarily any melodic structure implied at all (at least not much) in the execution of a harmonic pattern. The instrumentation of a musical piece is also completely separable from the piece's melodic, rhythmic, contrapuntal, and harmonic design. That design is equally separable from the piece's expressive intention, as I mentioned earlier, only the essential themes and the general style of their progressive deployment being really very expressive, and a good eighty or ninety per cent of the musical notes in any long work being what they are, and even being there at all, often, for reasons purely rhetorical. The particular way in which repetition and variation are employed in musical continuity is a matter of free choice by the composer. It is very little imposed by the nature of the music's desired expressive effect. And down to the most insignificant percussive tap or the most neutral harmonic filling, every separate pattern that contributes to the general collective pattern is a consistent musical pattern of some kind. If it isn't you get hubbub.

The proportion of expressive pattern to neutral pattern in any piece varies with local tradition. The Latins love abstraction and the Germanics love collective sentiment.

Consequently the Italian tendency is to put all the human expression into one place (the melody) and to frame that element with abstract music like scales, trills, arpeggios, and harmonic plunk-plunk, disposing these in a purely rhetorical, an architectural, way. The Germanics, horrified by this radical dissociation of elements and not really liking abstractions much anyway, accept the advantageous architectonics of the system, and then proceed to conceal these by spreading a rich layer of carefully adjusted expressiveness over all the subsidiary elements.

The Gallic, or French, musical procedure is less radically abstractionist than the Italian and less collectively expressive than the German, though it is predominantly Latin in its frank employment of dissociative methods. Its great contribution to European musical technique is its separation of muscular, or accentual, meter from prosodic, or quantitative, meter. This makes the French the world masters on the one hand of musical prose declamation and on the other, along with their Russian progeny, of ballet music. Also of a kind of musical landscape-painting that it is only possible to do when one can keep the piece static by separating quantitative rhythm from accentual intoxication.

Italian music tends by its abstraction to lack human expressiveness. German music has two besetting sins.

One is to get muddy through lack of a sufficiently delicate adjustment among the divers expressive elements; and the other is to go round and round, to get into waltz or march rhythms that put everybody into a narcotic state. The French trouble is overdoing the static, not seeming to get anywhere, because quantitative prose rhythms without much muscular whip-it-up in them are not very interesting to the blood-stream.

The marriage of these three traditions produced in Vienna between the years 1750 and 1850 the highest concentration of humanistic expression into musical form the Western world has ever known. That is history. That flowering is over, at least the best part of it. But the curve of decline is slow, as all historical evolutions are; new things will be under way long before Mozart and Beethoven are forgotten. I want to point out, though, as long as it is still possible to understand a bit the Viennese masters and what they had in their minds, that:

¶A. They practiced all the esoteric musical techniques, the canon, the fugue, prose declamation, imitative vocal counterpoint, and the air with Alberti bass;

¶B. They wrote in all the popular styles of song-and-dance music of all the European ethnic groups;

¶C. Although mostly star performers themselves, they never had improvisational mania or virtuoso disease. (Wagner, not a Viennese, caught the latter in Paris.)

¶D. They fused the popular manner with the esoteric techniques (always the aim of Western art) without ever sacrificing the force of one to the beauty of the other or obscuring the fact that the two are two.

Their technique itself was in the highest degree analytic, every element being completely dissociable from every other, both for instruction purposes and for practice. And texture was equally dissociable from expression. So much so that their greatest triumph was a kind of lengthy instrumental piece of a purely introspective nature which was nevertheless completely comprehensible (on sheer technical grounds) to interpreters and to consumers. They didn't even give these pieces titles or conceive them for any but purely musical usage. The nearest thing I know in any other art-work to the Viennese sonata-and-symphony literature is Cubist painting, and even that is at once less hermetic in construction and less popular in appeal.

This is because painting is a one-man job and doesn't have to be technically competent. Every man who works by himself gets either improvisational mania, which means a sacrifice of hieratic beauty to expression, a thing which is not hermetic at all (and beauty must be hermetic), or virtuoso disease, which means a sacrificing of both humane expression and hieratic beauty to streamlined execution; this, though it may make many a non-stop flight around the world, rarely arrives at being anything more than impressively expensive, rarely penetrates the dumb-bell human heart.

The Viennese musical apogee is long since over, though its tradition still goes on in slow decline. In its early decline it encountered certain foreign popular traditions on the up-grade, namely, those of the Spanish gypsies, the Hungarian gypsies, and the Russian gypsies. The confluence rejuvenated art-music a little, amplified these popular traditions a lot. The slight rejuvenation that took place in art-music between 1890 and 1914 was called Modern Music. Its centers were the ancient centers of esoteric musical knowledge, Vienna and Paris.

Art-music has made no advance since the war except for the grafting on of a few goat-glands from the Americas. Popular music, however, has made such advances in the United States that the swing-world today can almost be said to represent an art-tradition, with its academies, its pedagogues, its great men, its written histories, and some highly disinterested criticism. It was in a trade magazine of popular music that I recently found the following recipe for a proper musical performance. Jam, says Henry Dupre of New Orleans, should be played "from the heart, honestly, and for musicians only." Mr. Dupre is here advocating a higher standard of composition, as well as of performance (because jam is not merely execution) than I have ever seen advocated in any publication devoted to modern music of the high-brow schools.

Modern music has been for twenty-five years at such a standstill that musicians now practically all understand about it. Laymen, however, are still pretty confused. They are confused because they think it has something to do with modern poetry or with the modern painter's trick of multiple viewpoint. As I explained above, the discipline of mental dissociation is the oldest tradition in music. Also that music, for all the decay of Vienna, is still a collective art in all of its manifestations, high-brow and low-brow. Modern painting and poetry are two other stories. It may be that painting and poetry will hit the bottom of solitude soon and bounce up again into the collective practices. At the moment they are still one-man jobs. Their practitioners are trying to use analytic methods without objectivity and to be spontaneous in an epoch when there are no conventions left through which visual spontaneity can be made clear. There will be some possibility of comparing music with the visual and the verbal arts when these latter shall have become collective arts again, or when music shall have sunk to being made all alone in a room by one little man, who produces the sounds he wants to hear by electromagnetic means and records the whole on film without recourse to executants.

CHAPTER TWELVE

BACK TO POLITICS, or

How to run an island civilization

IT IS frequently proposed that artists and intellectuals should form a solid political front of some kind. I have seen a number of these movements in action, and I do not think musicians make much sense in them. Poets may.

One of the striking things about poets is their passion for collectivist theories of government. They have great disdain, however, for the collectively practiced arts. They are suspicious of architecture and the stage and just barely tolerate music for its possible advantages to poetry whenever some composer sets a few of their verses. Painting they accept if they can command its subject-matter.

They do lots of theorizing about the possible relations between solitary art and collective government. The leftist and revolutionary-minded wings are always getting together (sometimes with a painter or two along to give them the air of not being just a band of unemployed) and issuing manifestos. The sense of these manifestos is mostly something like this: that the chief function of art right now is to aid in bringing about a workers' revolution and that the chief business of the workers' revolutionary government will be to raise the economic and civil status of art-workers. This is a perfectly intelligible demand on their part, if by art and art-workers you understand poetry and poets. It is the natural and proper attitude of any group of persons among whom unemployment runs as high as it does among them. Such a demand would be absurd from members of the musical profession. Mark you that the private adherence of musicians to revolutionary (or anti-revolutionary or counter-revolutionary) political organizations is a legitimate thing and a very frequent thing. That need not bother anybody but our political masters. What is impossible to conceive is that the members of the musical trades and professions should give up a real economic status based on a wide, non-political function (I mean the supplying of music to its habitual consumers) for a non-paying economic status based at present on a narrow and sectarian function.

It is doubtful if music has any useful service to render

the Revolution right now. I have always noticed that workers' concerts, proletarian operas, and demonstrations of mass-singing tend to appease class hatreds and revolutionary fervors rather than to augment them. Also, the trades and professions at which people can (whether they actually do or not) earn a living furnish very few militants to revolutionary movements. What they do furnish to workers' organizations is lots of militant trade-unionists, all out, and very firmly out, for a quick amelioration of their own economic condition. Any musician who feels a need for changing things economically can get co-operation from other musicians and from all the trade-union groups, and he can change lots of things that way. That is a normal formula for effecting social reform and a quite powerful one. I cannot see that it would do the musician (employed or unemployed) any good to join up with the poets, all of whom are unemployed but none of whom have any tie-up (as poets) with the general labor federations.

The only known way for any craft or profession to raise its economic and civil status is by group action through its trade-unions and its professional bodies. Persons and groups who have no trade-union or effective professional body must essay to raise their condition by private means if any. The most common of these means is collaboration with political organizations whose function is to provoke radical political change. The adherence of musicians to such parties is a private matter and is usually kept so. The influence of such organizations on the policies of trade-unions and professional bodies is operated by interior pressure within those bodies. This is entirely legitimate. The rôle played by militant Marxian organizations in trade-union activity has never been very different from the rôle, for instance, that the Catholic Church and the various inter-denominational religious associations play in organized philanthropy, nor from the dominant rôle played in our institutions of learning by the representatives of banking and heavy industry that administer their funds. All that is a matter for trade-unions, social workers' groups, and educational foundations to handle from the inside. They do so handle it for the most part and present, in consequence, a united front to the public.

I have been attacked privately a good deal and once or twice in public gatherings for my unwillingness to announce a political affiliation of any kind, whether of an officially revolutionary or of an anti-revolutionary nature. So, I presume, have many other musicians. I continue to remain outside all that and shall continue to do so for the following reasons:

I believe that trade-unions and professional bodies must function as groups (and as groups of groups) with regard to changes in government and society. Any influence I may be able personally to exert over such transformations is, I think, more effective when operated through worker or professional solidarity. If my union or my professional body disagrees with me about any policy whose adoption I advocate, I can do one of two things. Either I can accept majority rule and shut up, or I can stage a little war. I can call the lay-public to my aid through the press and attempt to produce a change of opinion that way in enough of my colleagues to enable me to alter the previously taken attitude of my professional body. I cannot, however, continue very long manifesting in public my difference of opinion from that of my colleagues without rendering all of us ineffectual. Nothing is more legitimate and proper than that any citizen should have private political or religious affiliations which furnish him guidance in matters of private and even of professional conduct. Nothing is more suicidal, however, than to use one's professional prestige to give weight to public statements of private opinion.

There is no reason for my making a public statement of any kind excepting in my character as a professional musician. In that case I assume responsibility for my statements, and I accept correction of them from other musicians. If I use what professional prestige I have to advertise railways, pharmaceutical specialties, or international sources of ethical guidance, I submit myself to the public in the attitude of any banal celebrity whose interest to the public is just that of any other equally publicized character who may be a has-been tomorrow. I diminish the prestige of my whole profession by using my position in it for non-professional purposes, and I diminish my own influence within the profession by making public statements on matters either that do not regard the profession at all or about which the profession itself contains differences of opinion. Remember the horse-laugh that went up about all professors and scientists when forty of them in Germany (I think forty was the number) signed a manifesto during the Big War about who they thought should be allowed to win it. They had signed, I presume, on the naïve assumption that their professional distinction was sufficient to convince their colleagues in foreign countries that the German foreign policy of the moment was nobler than anybody else's.

Recently I was speaking of these matters with a poet of my acquaintance who has a certain knowledge of trade-union history and an elaborate knowledge of revolutionary theory. He explained to me that the musicians were quite right, from a revolutionary point of view, to maintain strong trade-unions and to demand every social and economic amelioration; that such action, when taken by organized trade-groups, did not constitute an advocacy of social reformism as a complete political program; that, on the contrary, strong unions were the best possible preparation for a well-working socialism. But when

I told him I had written in this book that professional composers were fools to do anything in public, on the strength of their professional reputation, that would tend to diminish the prestige of the whole profession by producing grave discord within it, and that consequently I recommended to composers just now to take their political action through their professional bodies, he accused me of advocating anarcho-syndicalism. It took me fifteen minutes to get it through his poet's wordy head that my advocacy of professional solidarity was in no way connected with any ism or with any messianic ideas about how a perfect state should function. I do not have any ideas, public or private, about the perfect state. I do not think professional people with a professional practice of any kind are likely to go in much for those ideal static structures. What we are much more likely to feel about political forms and their administration is that we shall have to defend our professional rights by eternal vigilance under any kind of government. We are willing to leave to Cæsar (if we must) everything politic and fiscal, though we shall grouse no end about that. We must demand, and, if we demand as a solid professional body, we shall obtain (and keep) from any governing agency of whatever kind in any possible state, both economic security for our members and the musical direction of all enterprises of whatever nature where music is employed.

I fancy that to this end collaboration between composers' professional bodies and the unions of executant musicians, which form, in turn, a part of the general labor federations, will in the long run be a more fruitful collaboration than the present pooling of interests between composers and publishers that is the operating basis of all the performing-rights societies. I think this for three reasons:

¶1. The present mechanism of our collaboration with publishers provides no means for adjudicating disputes between composers and publishers that arise from a disparity in their interests.

¶2. The publishers themselves, mostly small capitalists, are at any moment likely to find themselves owned by large banking and industrial pools. This development has already begun to take place. Warner Brothers own about half the publishers of popular music in the United States. And, as I mentioned earlier, Central-European performing rights are administered in America through an agency owned by North American Utilities. When an analogous situation shall have become general in music publishing, the only possible way for composers to obtain any recognition by publishers of their legitimate divergencies of interest will be through the aid of some equally powerful combination or organization. The general labor federations are the only non-capitalist organizations in existence that have that kind of power.

¶3. The performing-rights societies are private organizations that collect taxes from public and private musical enterprises. They are at present tolerated by most governments. Their position, however, in both law and equity is far more tenuous than that of the collective-bargaining associations. They are constantly being sued as combinations in restraint of trade and as profit-making organizations whose turn-over should be taxable by municipalities, states, and central governments. So far they seem to have resisted these attacks effectively, most of which are financed by radio companies, movie companies, and similar large tie-ups of electrical patents with banking. The minute the publishers shall have been bought out by these same tie-ups, any association of composers and publishers will be just a company union for the electrical recording-and-transmission combines.

Do not think that I am proposing an industrial union of all music-workers. I don't think that would be a bad idea for executant musicians, copyists, arrangers, musical engravers, teachers, and persons who make musical instruments. Such a development seems to be taking place in America through the American Federation of Musicians (actually a craft-union, but moving rapidly toward the absorption of all music-workers). I should approve highly of such a union, but I do not see much place in it for composers, excepting in so far as these may be also pianists or teachers or some other kind of time worker. Because, in spite of all the community of interests and of understanding that exists between the composers and the other musicians, the fact remains that workers who work under somebody else's direction, executing somebody else's plan, and getting paid for it by the hour, have a completely different view of life and a different set of financial interests from persons who work privately, time not being of the essence at all, and who get paid for a piece of work not on a basis of how long that work took to get written but on the basis of how long it takes to play it and how many people listen, who get paid proportionally, that is, to the usage their work receives.

I do not say that it might not be a good idea for governments to guarantee a minimum living to all citizens, composers included. That would be an act of general amelioration which it might be possible to put into effect, though I don't think it ever has been attempted anywhere. It might be equally desirable to limit the profits from professional work to a reasonable figure by slapping super-taxes on composers' incomes. (Don't laugh. Successful authors of all kinds in Soviet Russia make astronomical sums.) Those are extreme but perfectly imaginable social measures. It is difficult to imagine, however, short of a complete socialization of society where nobody got paid for anything, any way of making just compensation to musical authors for the public exploitation of their work (in case any such exploitation takes place and for any reason and by means of no matter what financial backing) on any other basis than that of a fee proportional to the time occupied in performance and to the number of persons listening.

The chief characteristics of professional men are their economic independence and their intellectual authority. That authority and that independence are obtained by never charging the customer for preparation, experiment, or correction but by accepting payment only for professional services rendered. Different kinds of work are measurable for payment in different ways. The time a composer actually takes to write a given piece is not a reasonable or possible way of measuring that work's commercial value. Its value for payment must be measured by its utility, as all professional services are.

Consequently, the composer would be foolish to submit his economic destiny and the protection of his professional interests to any federation of mere musical workmen, at least 99.99 per cent of whose work is measurable for paying purposes by the time they spend doing it. The high-powered soloists and conductors are a little more like us than the anonymous instrumentalists are. They prepare privately, accept in their own name responsibility for public failure, and charge what the market will bear. But even these glamorous characters are not independent and authoritative workmen. They execute somebody else's design, usually on order. Any freedom they have about repertory (even about style) exists only within the narrow limits predetermined by managers. It would not be proper for a composers' professional body to accept any direction whatever from, or any equality in voting with, professional inferiors.

A professional body is not a trade-union. There is every reason for the professional body at certain periods of history to obtain economic privileges from or through the exploiting classes. There is every reason that I know of in this period to obtain and to expect to keep on obtaining what we want through collaboration with our executant workmen, who are better organized than we are and who, if they aren't any stronger than the exploiting classes, are in a little better position to aid us in securing performances and in getting paid for them than the exploiters are. This may seem strange, but it is true none the less. Because the executants have an interest in the continual performance by hand of lots and lots of music, whereas the exploiters' principal interest today lies in the widest possible dissemination of reproductions of the smallest possible amounts of actual musical performance. Whether in the long run the reproduction-systems are beneficial to the musical art remains to be seen. It looks right now as if the executant musicians have, on the whole, more to offer composers than the owners of electrical patents have.

In any case, although I personally favor the collaboration of composers' bodies with musical trade-unions (even to the point of the closed shop, provided the composers' professional body keeps itself open to all composers of every school and reasonable degree of proficiency) rather than with finance-capital, I do maintain that the professional bodies, all professional bodies, doctors, engineers, architects, and the rest, must remain independent bodies, ready at all times to defend their intellectual and economic independence from all organizations of persons not practicing that profession as original designers. This is the only professional policy likely to ensure the survival of the major techniques through changes in government and administration. And I maintain that that preservation, cultivation, and transmission of the autonomous techniques through changes in government and administration that are the mark of the great civilizations are a desirable thing for everybody connected with any civilization.

The professional bodies nourish their traditions by the pooling of private knowledge and by the transmission of this knowledge esoterically to persons of (or potentially of) the profession. The consolidation and transmission of professional knowledge is a permanent function. Disseminating the fruits of this knowledge varies with public need and taste. Music is tolerated, regulated, sometimes slightly encouraged by governments, by private capital, and by workmen's protective associations. Sometimes no attention is paid to it at all. On the whole and in the long run, the professional man's working life is indissolubly bound up with his professional colleagues and with the general public, not with governments, not with members of the other professions, not with the social needs of any particular class among his co-citizens. The composer works at his best and society profits from him most not only when he writes music "from the heart, honestly, and for musicians only" but when he takes what political action he takes as the member of an indissoluble professional body.

Everybody nowadays wants to dictate the social usages of art. The authoritarian governments are on the warpath to make art serve their foreign policy or their social theories. The revolutionists are doing their best to subject the Beautiful Arts to summary judgment by persons unknown. A lot of unemployed workers in the solitary arts, chiefly poets, are trying to get a job by turning their talent as dialecticians to the speeding up of political and social change, because they know that a political revolution of collectivist character is more likely to bring them a public again than is any minor amelioration of the status quo.

There is not yet any analogous movement in music, even in the United States, where musicians' unemployment runs high. If the American Federation of Musicians and the American Guild of Musical Artists and the American Composers' Alliance are still not entirely the secular arm of international politics or of any pool of bankers, philanthropists, and trustees, that is not because their leadership is superior or their membership dumb. It is because in the Western world Music is still a going concern. In spite of the decay of the Viennese tradition and the growth of the Appreciation-racket, music still gets written, performed, and consumed, lots of it, in all categories. And neither the profession of writing it nor the trade of performing it is quite yet immobilized by friction with the businessmen who organize the dissemination of it.

The island world, for all the physical poverty and mental pretentiousness of its leaders, for all the real suffering that exists among the executants, for all the outrageous designs of finance-capital on consumers' taste and authors' pocketbooks, the island civilization still functions in the world as an integrated civilization, an auditive civilization, the only civilization to which persons whose viscera are strongly audito-sensitive can ever possibly give whole-hearted allegiance.